Praise For *Awakening from Grief*

"This book is exactly what you need to read to heal your aching heart . . . it will feel like a warm shower running inside of you where coldness previously lived . . . BEAUTIFULLY WRITTEN!"

Dr. Wayne W. Dyer
Author, *Your Erroneous Zones,*
Your Sacred Self, Real Magic

"A MUST READ for the soul. If you are grieving, this book will comfort you. If not, it will prepare you for that which is not small stuff."

Richard Carlson, Ph.D.
Author, *Don't Sweat the Small Stuff*

"Everyone experiences grief. My great friend John Welshons has insights that will source and serve you, get you through your pain, and mend your broken heart. I love the great thinking in this book!"

Mark Victor Hansen
Co-Creator, New York Times #1 Best-Selling Series,
Chicken Soup for the Soul

"OUTSTANDING! . . . Very moving . . . John's heart, his years of experience, and his expertise show through clearly on every page of this excellent book.

The path of grief is full of twists and turns. John accompanies the reader, torch in hand . . . hand in hand . . . along that path.

There is a healing to be found in grief. Guideposts are within Awakening From Grief."

Stephen and Ondrea Levine
Authors, *A Year to Live, Who Dies?*
Embracing the Beloved

Awakening from Grief

Finding the road back to joy.

John E. Welshons

Open Heart
Publications

Little Falls, New Jersey

Published by OPEN HEART PUBLICATIONS
P.O. Box 110
Little Falls, New Jersey 07424
www.openheartseminars.com
e-mail: jwelshon@ix.netcom.com

Publisher's Cataloging-in-Publication Data
Welshons, John E.
     Awakening from grief: finding the road back to joy / John E.
     Welshons – Little Falls, New Jersey : Open Heart Publications., 2000.
          p.   cm.
     ISBN 1-928732-57-7

     1. Grief. 2. Loss. (Psychology) I. Title.
BF575.G7 W45   2000   99-64741
152.4   dc—21   CIP

Cover design by Turchette Advertising Agency, Fairfield, New Jersey
PROJECT COORDINATION BY JENKINS GROUP, INC.

03 02 01 00 ▲ 5 4 3 2 1

Printed in the United States of America

This book is dedicated with deepest gratitude to my parents, Flo and Al Welshons, whose extraordinary sharing of their lives, their confusions, their pain, their joy, their grief, and ultimately their deaths gave me the foundation for all of this work.

To Ram Dass, whose teaching, friendship, and love have given me more than any other individual in this lifetime.

To Stephen and Ondrea Levine, who have shown me what true love and compassion are, who have allowed me to experience what true "family" really is. To Ondrea for being the original inspiration for this book.

To Meher Baba who showed me who we really are, who taught me that "Real happiness lies in making others happy."

To Charlie Garfield, who first helped me open my mind and heart to my own grief . . . who first introduced me to the joy and honor of working with others on theirs.

To Elisabeth Kubler-Ross, who with great compassion and wisdom helped us all to take our heads out of the sand.

To Allan Y. Cohen, whose "simple prescription" has served me well for twenty-six years.

To Pascal Kaplan for creating that amazing conference in Berkeley, California in 1976. It changed my life.

To Tom Decker for first telling me about the conference and advising me to go . . . and for being my spiritual brother for all these years.

To Mark Victor Hansen, whose encouragement led me to do what I really want to do.

To Robert T. Latimer, who helped me break free of the prison of my past . . . who showed me that I am much bigger and much more creative than I ever dreamed possible.

To Charles E. Gauntt, who whenever I said, "I can't" said, "Yes, you can!"

To Bill Bates for his friendship, and for bringing a much-needed new perspective to an industry that serves people at the most difficult time of their lives.

To Patricia Hunt-Perry, for her steadfast friendship and for her early comments on this book which helped to shape it into something that might be really useful to others.

To Gary Horn for his incredible ability to turn loss and grief into growth and awareness . . . for being one of the greatest inspirations in my life.

To my sisters Judy and Carole, who have shared their amazing capacities for love, and who have worked through the extraordinarily painful losses in their own lives with dignity, wisdom, and courage.

To Jan Bonial, Mabel Dobbins, Ed Lavoie, Armando Lopez, Betsy Lowe, Cynthia Maltese, Ted Hershey, Claudia Moroz-Valentini, Francis Murray, Bruce Nagy, Ed O'Deven, Tom Veenendall, Venna Welshons, Fred Winterfeldt, Joe and Edith Zales, and all of the other amazing beings who have allowed me an intimate view into their noble, heartful, and graceful deaths.

To Colleen Adomaitis, Beth Counseller, Janie Cress, Ron Bonial, Marion Brozowski, Carol Caunter, Martin Colverd, Andy and Andrea Conroy, Colleen Dore, Pat Downey, Karen Eramo, Ben Gambardella, Diane Gillespie, Laura Glenn Hershey, Carrie Joyce, Dawn Laboc, Heidi Mastrogiovanni, Jackie, Michelle, and Rosa Moroz, Jay and Beverly Maltese, Sam and Arden McCleskey, John, Maureen, Sharon, Kathleen, and Pat Murray, Randy Niederer, Adele Pingree, Michael Redmond, Pat Santini, Gay Sherman, Gail Stern, Janet Steyermark, Todd Van Beck, Nick Valentini, Wilhelmina Walton, Dave White, Dennis Woolard, and all of the other amazing beings who have allowed me a glimpse into their grief, and have inspired me with their ability to allow grief to open their hearts so that they might find a deeper, fuller, more meaningful experience of life and love.

To John Mazzoni, Tom Rushforth, and the wonderful staff of The Hilton at Short Hills . . . Alf, Ana, Brian, Armando, Charity, Chris, Gerald, Gertrude, Gregory, Ioane, James, Joey, Kay, Lisa, Marvin, Melissa, Nadia, Orlando, Richard, Rosa, Sam, Sharon, Tony . . . and everyone else. The peace, solace, and friendship they provided during my extended retreats there in 1998 and 1999 created a wonderfully calm and supportive environment in which most of this was written . . .

And to Sammy, who reminded us all . . .

ACKNOWLEDGMENTS

In the past, when I have seen the following list in books, I have never so fully understood its importance. But, quite clearly, this book could not have become what it is without the assistance of so many people who read early versions and gave so generously of their time and insight. These are true friends who helped me shape this book into what it is today. This is their book as much as mine:

First and foremost, Lori Katterhenry, for nineteen years of deep friendship and partnership, for her love, wisdom, insight and support during many of the events portrayed in this book, and for helping me learn how to move my writing from my mind to my heart.

I also wholeheartedly thank Linda Acorn, Leslie Dennen, Charlie Garfield, Earl Grollman, Patricia Hunt-Perry, Jerry Jenkins, Stephen and Ondrea Levine, Laurie Matarazzo, Chris and Barbara Montan, Nils and Teresa Montan, Maureen Murray, Steve Morgan, Theresa Nelson, Michael Redmond, David Shipper, Aaron Shipper, Nikki Stahl, and Todd Van Beck, for taking the time to make thoughtful, insightful comments that vastly improved the quality of this book.

Finally, I thank Jim Gorab, Chuck Nussman, and Walter Joyce at Turchette Advertising in Fairfield, New Jersey, for their beautiful cover design, and for always helping me quickly and efficiently in so many, many ways.

CONTENTS

Contents

*It is difficult to think of dying
consciously when we notice how incomplete we feel, how
frightened we are of life. It is almost as though we
were never completely born . . .*

STEPHEN LEVINE,
IN *Who Dies?*

PREFACE

ONE BEAUTIFUL, SUNNY AFTERNOON IN MARCH OF 1976, I HAD A startling, life-changing realization.

I was sitting in a classroom on the campus of John F. Kennedy University in Orinda, California attending a five-day conference entitled "Perspectives on Death, Dying, and . . . Beyond . . ." Charlie Garfield was presenting a workshop on counseling people who were terminally ill.

I had originally gone to the conference because I was interested in the ". . . Beyond . . ." I was a student of world religions, and was fascinated by different models of afterlife.

Although I had already been touched by death and loss many times in my life, I had embraced our culture's commitment to ignoring the difficult emotions that are brought on by loss. I had learned how to intellectualize the process. I looked for solace in the hope of a "better hereafter."

But despite my intellectual hunger for fascinating, inspirational theories about what happens to us *after* dying, Charlie Garfield, in his keynote presentation, spoke more about the experience of working with people who were *in the process* of dying and *in the process* of grieving than he did about what happens to us *after* death.

Elisabeth Kubler-Ross, the other keynote speaker at the conference, had done exactly the same thing.

Frankly, I didn't really want to hear it.

But I couldn't help being deeply moved. Elisabeth and Charlie's stories of working with people who were dying and people in grief portrayed a depth of human connection I had never previously experienced.

Working with loss, grief, and death were things our culture considered impossibly painful and difficult . . . things most people wanted neither to talk about or think about.

Yet Elisabeth and Charlie were two of the most fully alive and fully human beings I had ever encountered.

They had so many special qualities; such deep compassion, such profound honesty, such extraordinary willingness to look at the most difficult aspects of life and death. And what amazed me most was their profound insight into how we can use these difficult experiences in order to learn how to live.

Something inside me said, "Whatever it is they're doing, I want to do it, too."

And as Charlie guided us through a visualization about confronting our own death, I began to realize that I had a tremendous fear around the issue of death. And I realized that my fear had never been alleviated by belief in the afterlife.

Then I realized that it *couldn't* be alleviated by belief in the afterlife. It had nothing to do with the afterlife. *It was a fear of life.* It was a fear about not living. It was the startling realization that if I had been given a terminal diagnosis by my doctor that day, I would have been devastated. I would have felt that in twenty-five years of *being alive*, I had never really *lived*.

I looked at all my relationships and felt a profound sadness as I realized how *incomplete* they all felt . . . how frightened I was of intimacy . . . how many walls I had constructed to keep people out of my heart.

I looked at my commitment to my goals, to my dreams, to my spiritual life, and realized how lukewarm it had all been . . . I realized that although I appeared to be intelligent, and alive, I had been stumbling around in a fog much of my life.

I realized that if I had died that day, I would have died feeling that I had never really known . . . had never really touched . . . had never really felt deep love and commitment. I would have died feeling that I had never experienced life.

To the extent that we hold ourselves back from living life fully, we will fear death . . . and we will fear the deaths of our loved ones . . . and we will fear loss.

And when loss comes, we are devastated because of all of the ways we failed to experience . . . failed to commit to . . . failed to fully appreciate that person, that relationship, that aspect of our life that is now gone.

What held us back was fear.

What locks us in grief is more fear. The fear that our life will never be the same after loss . . . that we will never get over the loneliness . . . that we will never find real meaning in life . . . that we will never fill the void . . . that somehow we could have done something to prevent the loss.

This book is about going beyond fear and becoming fully alive.

And the first part of that process is the willingness to look at the losses in our lives, and our reactions to them, openly and honestly.

A few years ago I published a series of articles on grief in a professional trade journal. I had intended to write from a relatively academic perspective.

But what came through me when I sat down at the computer was a number of personal stories of loss and how those losses affected my life.

I was a little apprehensive about publishing the stories. But the editor liked them. And when they were published, many readers called to tell me how much *they* liked them. I would ask what they liked best. "Your personal stories!" they would say.

So what I offer to you in *Awakening from Grief* is those stories . . .

and several others . . . woven together with strands of awareness that comprise the essence of my understanding about grief and loss.

I now realize that from the time I was a child I was having experiences that were preparing me for this work.

It is my hope that you will find many points of connection . . . that you will realize these are not just *my* stories, but *our* stories. Many of you will have similar stories. They are stories of the difficult events that shape us, that exert profound, monumental influence over our lives . . . and yet are seldom discussed in "polite company."

I am convinced that our reluctance to look clearly at these kinds of events is what keeps us stuck in grief. It's what keeps us from fully experiencing our lives.

I hope that you will find this open, honest exploration useful in your own growth. I hope that this book will help you to "awaken," to live your life, to love your life, and to love your loved ones fully, openly, and exuberantly . . . to heal through the losses you have experienced, and to feel more prepared for the losses to come.

May your life be filled with many blessings . . . the blessing of love . . . the blessing of peace . . . the blessing of joy . . . the blessing of healing . . . the blessing of finding *the joy inside your tears!*

John E. Welshons
Little Falls, New Jersey
August 1999

FOREWORD

THE LOSSES IN OUR LIVES ARE THE HARDEST THINGS WE HAVE TO FACE . . .
A loved one dies . . .
A relationship ends . . .
We lose a job, a friend, a treasured dream . . .
A child is ill . . .
We lose our physical health, or ability . . .
And . . .

Our world turns upside down.

We lose our bearings. We lose our joy. We lose our security.

We no longer know who we are. We no longer know what our life is about. We no longer trust.

We long for something to take away the pain . . . to change the circumstance . . . to bring back the one we love . . . to return us, and our lives, to wholeness.

For many of us, the question is, "How do I begin again? How do I find happiness again?"

For others, the only real question is, "When will this pain end?"

If we can look at the losses in our lives a little differently . . . if we can change our perspective just slightly . . . we may see that within this experience lie the seeds of a new beginning . . . of a new life . . . of a deeper experience of love and fulfillment than we ever imagined possible.

We may see that
When our heart is broken . . .
It is also *wide open.*

We may find that
No matter how devastated we feel . . .
There is still *boundless joy to be found in our heart.*

This book is about changing perception . . .

It is about healing the losses we have already experienced, and preparing for the inevitable losses to come.

It is about learning to see the pain of loss as a gift . . .

A gift we didn't ask for . . .

But . . .

Here it is.

Loss is an inevitable part of being human

And our choice is either to remain in pain and bitterness . . .

Or . . .

To learn how to use this experience to grow into a richer, more fulfilling life.

In that sense loss is a gift,
A gift that will open our hearts . . .
If we let it . . .
A gift that can help us uncover the extraordinary LOVE we always hoped, but never dared imagine, is within us.
It is about finding JOY again.

Awakening from Grief

Each person who enters our life,
and every experience we have
is a teacher.
Some things we learn about ourselves
amaze us.
Some trouble us.

But through it all,
each relationship continues . . .
Everyone we have loved
has become a part of us . . .
And no relationship,
created in love,

can ever die . . .

Chapter One

BEING FULLY ALIVE AND FULLY HUMAN

People say that what we are seeking is a meaning for life. I don't think that's what we're really seeking. I think that what we're seeking is an experience of being alive, so that we actually feel the rapture of being alive.

JOSEPH CAMPBELL

IN THE MIDST OF EMOTIONAL PAIN, IT'S DIFFICULT TO IMAGINE EVER being happy.

It's difficult to see anything positive or hopeful.

The world looks bleak, dark, and dreary.

Our heart hurts with a deep, relentless ache.

All we want is to have our life, our body, our heart, returned to fullness . . . to have our loved one back . . . to heal the hurt . . .

To heal our wounded heart.

We wouldn't ask for experiences that hurt so much.

We wonder what kind of a God would create a Universe where such sadness is possible.

But these experiences are an inevitable part of being human.

We live in a culture which has sought to protect us from sadness.
But we live in a world where sadness is inevitable.
So we have a problem.

Every time someone has said to you, "Don't cry. Be strong. Keep a stiff upper lip. Don't think about that. Let's talk about something more pleasant. Here, have a drink, you'll feel better," they have taught you not to grieve.

These messages have come from our parents, our siblings, our teachers, our friends, and, for the most part, they have been given with the best of intentions. They have been given with the hope that our lives will be happier if we distract ourselves from sadness.

But, inevitably, we find out that isn't possible.

And we usually find that out when something cataclysmic happens . . . when we suffer a loss that is greater than all the other losses. A loss we can't ignore. A sadness we can't subdue.

Then all the buried sadness from the other losses in our lives rises to the surface like an endless emotional volcano.

We quickly shift into numbness. The feelings are too overwhelming. They are too big. We fear we can't contain them all. So we turn them off.

We stagger around in an emotional stupor, only partially alive, filled with sorrow, anger, confusion, and despair.

The numbness is a natural process. It is similar to the state of shock our body goes into after a serious physical trauma.

But when we turn off our sadness, we also turn off our joy. If we turn off our feelings at one level, we turn them off at all levels. Then we don't feel fully alive.

Eventually, the challenge is to come out of the numbness.

It's difficult to do. Because each time we let down the barrier and allow ourselves to feel, we move right back into sadness, despair, and anger. Joy is nowhere to be found.

But peace, love, and joy exist — always — in the heart, just
beneath the despair, confusion, and anger. The perplexing reali-
ty is that the only route to joy is through the despair, confusion,
and anger. Being fully alive requires us to be willing to feel it all.

The world's great religions offer us some extremely helpful
images.

The Christian tradition refers to "The Sacred Heart of Jesus."

And what is that "Sacred Heart?"

It might be seen as a vast nurturing womb of love and compassion
. . . an immense, infinite fountain of healing and forgiveness for all
human suffering, all human failing . . . the sacred space where love
and compassion meet suffering.

Those beautiful meditative statues of Buddha, so common in people's homes and gardens, provide another useful insight into the real
challenge of human life.

He is peaceful . . . still . . . meditative . . . sitting cross-legged in the
lotus posture. . . quieting to hear the inner wisdom . . . to feel his full
awareness.

In that state of quietness, peace, and inner awareness, a subtle
smile radiates on his face.

His smile is known as "The smile of unbearable compassion." It is
the smile that sees it all, the smile that radiates from within his being.
He is fully aware of all of the world's suffering. Still he smiles.

Nothing is hidden. Nothing is ignored. Nothing is overlooked.

He sees all of the suffering clearly. He drinks it in. He under-
stands its root cause. He experiences unending compassion. He has
made it his life's purpose to alleviate human suffering.

And still he smiles.

His joy exists within the fullness of the human experience. And
the fullness of the human experience includes both joy and suffering . . . both loss and gain . . . both sadness and laughter.

These elements of our beings are not mutually exclusive. We do
not have to push one away in order to feel the other.

The full experience of being human is to feel all of them existing within us at all times.

The challenge of being human is to find that "Sacred Heart" within ourselves, to smile "the smile of unbearable compassion," to give ourselves and others love, compassion, and forgiveness in the midst of devastating loss and grief.

Our society, in seeking to protect us from that which is unpleasant, effectively left us unprepared for loss and sadness.

Our work now is to begin learning that which our society hoped we wouldn't have to learn. It is to learn how to be whole, to be loving, and to be happy living in a world of unpredictable, often uncontrollable, change.

Chapter Two

THE TEACHINGS OF LOSS

Life is what happens to you
while you're busy making other plans.
JOHN LENNON

AFTER TWENTY-FIVE YEARS OF COUNSELING PEOPLE WHO ARE DYING and people in grief, one thing has become absolutely clear: Most of us spend much of our lives sleepwalking.

Even when we are frantically active, a part of us is usually sleeping.

That part is our full awareness, the awareness that observes and absorbs all of life, in its totality . . . both the joy and the sadness. The part of us that *sees it all,* all the time.

At some level it is the frantic pace of our modern life that forces us to keep that part asleep.

At another level it is the result of decades of cultural training.

Our culture encourages us to avoid looking squarely at the realities of human life.

We live our lives on "autopilot."

We busy ourselves with "the daily grind."

We distract ourselves with television and other forms of entertainment. We numb ourselves with alcohol and drugs.

We seek happiness in externals—in other people and external conditions.

We seek fulfillment in the acquisition of material objects and possessions.

We look into the eyes of others to tell us who we are, to affirm our worth and value.

And that conditioning leads us to keep postponing our lives, thinking that if we do what needs to be done today, if we meet all our responsibilities now, happiness and fulfillment will come later:

> When we can drive a car . . .
> When we go to college . . .
> When we fall in love . . .
> When we get married . . .
> When we have children . . .
> When we buy the dream house . . .
> When we buy the dream car . . .
> When the children get through college . . .
> When the children get married . . .
> When the children have children . . .
> When we get a new job . . .
> When we lose fifty pounds . . .
> When we have enough money in the bank . . .
> When the therapy begins to work . . .
> When he or she comes back to us . . .
> When we retire . . .
> When we recover from surgery . . .
> When someone we love recovers from addiction . . .
> On and on it goes.

We postpone fulfillment. We postpone joy. We postpone happiness. We allow our inner feelings to be dictated by external people and circumstances.

Our hearts tell us to give more attention to our loved ones . . . to give more attention to our inner selves . . . to our unique sense of purpose . . . to our secret yearnings, and our special talents.

But we ignore our hearts.
And we ignore our intuition.

We rationalize our lack of attention by telling ourselves we will take care of these things later. When life calms down, when more of our ideal life—as we imagine it to be—is in place, we will make up for neglecting these aspects of our life now.

Later we will have time for family.
Later we will have time for our selves.
Later we will be fulfilled.

Then suddenly, unexpectedly, *CHANGE* comes . . .
Sometimes in the form of illness.
Sometimes in the form of death.
Sometimes in the form of divorce.
And our whole world looks different.

Unfortunately, many of us will be shaken into wakefulness only by some cataclysmic event.

And it doesn't have any correlation to age.

Some people live into their seventies and eighties and yet approach death wondering what their life was all about, amazed at how quickly it all passed. They say, "I never thought about this happening. I thought I was going to live *forever*. I always thought I was going to be happy *later*. I always thought my life was something that was *about* to happen."

Others face the end of their time on earth with a sense of fulfillment, gratitude, and completion.

I have seen people in their teens, twenties, and thirties working effectively with a debilitating emotional or physical injury.

And I have seen people in their teens, twenties, and thirties face their own death or the death of someone they love. Quite often they come through the experience pulsating with life, enthusiasm, and hope. No matter how difficult the circumstances of their lives have been, they find a way to be fulfilled.

I have seen other people in their teens, twenties, and thirties in good health and relatively secure economic circumstances, embittered and despairing about the ways life has disappointed them. At some level, it's as if they are already dead.

What is the difference?

And how can we learn to use the difficulties and losses in our lives to open more fully, to open our hearts more fully, to pulsate with life, enthusiasm, and hope rather than closing our hearts and numbing our souls?

How do we keep from drowning in sadness?

Chapter Three

DEATHS AND REBIRTHS

We do not see things as they are.
We see them as we are.

THE TALMUD

MOST OF US WANT TO LIVE HAPPY LIVES.

We want peace and stability. We don't want difficulties.

But the difficult experiences in life are the ones that really cause us to grow.

We may not ask for these experiences. We may not want this growth.

But here it is.

We have no choice.

The difficult experiences capture our attention. They consume our awareness. They change our perspective.

They often force us to see ourselves differently . . . to live our lives differently.

They bring us face to face with our fears.

They give us exactly what we don't want.

The difficulties in our lives can wake us up . . . *if we let them.*

In that sense, death and loss have been the greatest teachers in my life.

Perhaps they can be for you, too.

They have taught me the significance of every day . . . the preciousness of each relationship . . . the need to stop postponing what is important.

They have forced me to explore deeper and deeper levels of love and acceptance.

They have forced me to learn that love and relationship exist beyond the limits and constraints of the body.

But they are fierce teachers. And like the other great teachers I have had, they have pushed and prodded me, sometimes ruthlessly, to gain a deeper understanding of who and what I am.

They have forced me to deepen my understanding of what life is about. They have brought me more and more into the moment. They have helped me to learn what love really is.

A raging storm of emotion is triggered by the loss of something or someone we love. And in that storm we feel unprepared to navigate the turbulent waters of our own grief.

Sometimes grief is so overwhelming that we panic, we go into a kind of "emotional shock." We become numb. At times we say, "I don't feel anything."

Hours, days, and weeks go by. It's all a blur. We feel "disconnected," like we're watching our life through a hazy fog. It doesn't seem to add up to anything. Whatever peacefulness and security we once had has been shattered by an inevitable reality we've spent our lives running away from.

At other times, in other circumstances, we feel panic. We rage against the seeming injustice of it all. We cry, we sob, we pound our fists. We feel a pain that is all-consuming. Our hearts are breaking. Our minds feel violated. "Why, why, why?" We ask, but no one answers.

Our friends, family, clergy and counselors try to answer, but it all seems contrived, useless, unrelated to what we feel.

The teachings of death and loss involve much more than the grief that follows a physical death or separation.

Every loss in our life forces us, to some extent, to re-experience the grief we have carried with us for all of life's unresolved losses.

My own life has been profoundly affected by many different losses.

When I was three, I had polio. I lost the opportunity to have a normal childhood. A part of me died.

Because of the polio I was a terrible athlete. Every time I failed to "make the team," every time a classmate ridiculed me on the athletic field, every time I found myself face down in the football field mud, a part of me died.

My most cherished companion, a beagle named "Punkin," died when I was ten. And a part of me died.

My father became an alcoholic when I was eleven. My idol, my hero, my role model turned into a raging demon . . . and a part of me died.

Vicious, screaming battles between my parents became a nightly ritual . . . and a part of me died.

On my twelfth birthday, my favorite baby-sitter was hit and killed by a car while crossing the street. She was on her way to my birthday party. A part of me died.

Later that year, I saw a boy my own age drown in the surf in Puerto Rico. His lifeless corpse was dragged onto the beach, his vacant, bloodshot eyes wide open but not seeing. His salt-parched body was covered with sand. He died, and a part of me died.

We came to the brink of nuclear war with Russia in 1962, and a part of me died.

Our president was murdered in 1963 and a part of me died,

When I was fourteen I didn't pass the audition for a rock band I really wanted to join. A part of me died.

The next day another boy was cast in a theatrical role I really wanted, and a part of me died.

When I was sixteen, my first love left me to date someone else, and a part of me died.

And as those deaths added up and added up, with no tools to process the feelings and no wisdom to integrate them into my life, each loss became another stone in a thick, hard wall that surrounded my heart.

So when I was seventeen, I left my second love because I could feel nothing. She loved me with a vibrant, nourishing, heartfelt love. But I felt nothing. Too much of me had died.

A few months later, when my mother was diagnosed with cancer of the colon, I again felt nothing. And it only occurred to me in passing that something was amiss, that my reaction, or lack thereof, was not what "normal" people would feel.

I loved my mother dearly. But her life with my father had become a tortured nightmare. At an earlier age the possibility that my mother might die was my greatest fear. But now I felt nothing. Perhaps it was just one too many tragedies for me to cope with.

> *Ironically, it was my mother's death that finally tore away the veil of numbness I had hidden behind for so many years. It gave me the first inkling that the parts of me that were dying were paving the way for a much more profound "birth."*

Fear, doubt, and anger were mysteriously, almost magically, replaced with an intuitive sense that everything was "all right" — that there was an underlying order to this seemingly random, chaotic, sometimes malevolent Universe. Where that intuition came from, how I finally tapped into it, and the manner in which it has grown in my life will all be explored in the pages of this book.

Suffice it to say that *I now know* that death and loss can be our greatest teachers. They are our greatest teachers because, in tearing away the people, the possessions, the hopes, and dreams we all cling to, they offer us the opportunity to find out who we really are . . . to discover the depths of our being . . . to know that which lies beyond our attachment to external people, places, and things . . . to know that, in all of us, which transcends death and loss. In that process, we have the opportunity to find *real and lasting happiness.*

Contemporary behavioral scientists talk about our "authentic self" or "inner being." And most religions refer to our "soul." But do any of us really know what they are talking about? Probably very few.

In the face of profound loss, so much of what we know ourselves to be and so much of what we know our life to be is torn away. We have the opportunity to glimpse, perhaps for the first time, what it is in each of us that underlies the roles, relationships, and abilities by which we have defined ourselves. *We may even have the opportunity to glimpse our own soul.*

Make no mistake, it is a painful process. There are moments of emotional despair in loss that we wouldn't wish on our worst enemy.

But birth is always painful. And profound loss can pave the way for a new birth, a new beginning, a recognition of something much more substantial than we have ever known previously . . . an unshakable awareness of our "inner being . . ." an introduction to that in each of us which is, in Ram Dass' words, *"invulnerable to the winds of changing time and space."*

> *In that invulnerable inner place,*
> *we come to know what it is in each of us*
> *that can never be lost, and can never die.*
> *We find at last, in our own hearts,*
> *the source of all happiness.*
> *We find the dwelling place of Love.*
> *We find the home of our loved ones,*
> *both living and dead.*
> *We find our Self.*

Chapter Four

AUNT MABEL

I WASN'T READY FOR ANY OF THIS.

No one close to me had died before.

But just three days after my twelfth birthday, we were on our way to say good-bye to Aunt Mabel.

She wasn't a "real" aunt. She was my favorite baby-sitter. My grandmother had met her on the train one day.

And, although I was twelve and she was seventy-two, she was my first real love.

She and I had hit it off several years earlier, the first time she came to our house. There was just something about her. I thought about her all the time. I talked to her on the phone for hours each day. I rode my bike over to her house whenever I could. Sometimes I rode back and forth past her house, even if she wasn't home, just to feel close to her.

She was warm and sweet and graceful and elegant. She always seemed happy to see me or hear from me.

She had wonderfully interesting stories about her parents, her child-hood, her husband, and her son.

I don't remember any of the stories, but I do remember sitting and listening, enraptured by her presence and grace.

She always seemed upbeat and positive. She believed in me, and she believed in life.

She lived a very simple life with her sister, Jess, in the upstairs part of a two-family house in Newark. Aunt Mabel had been widowed for some time. I don't think Jess had ever married.

They had none of the trappings of wealth and success by which I had been surrounded all my life.

In fact, I don't think I had ever seen anyone live in such a small space — a flight of stairs up to a small living room, a small kitchen, two small bedrooms, and a small bathroom.

And there were strangers living downstairs. It was an unusual contrast to the large mansion-like home my family lived in. Oddly enough, as I think back on it, there were strangers living in our house, too. But we were all related.

Aunt Mabel's apartment was furnished with big, old, clumsy furniture that didn't really fit. The decor didn't matter, though, because the house always seemed to be filled with light, serenity, peace, and joy.

In a very short time, Aunt Mabel became the most important person in my life. She taught me so much about strength of spirit and character and about living life with dignity and gratitude.

My parents had recently started drinking again. Our home was no longer fun, or safe.

But Mabel was wise and steady, an adult I could trust. I would tell her when my parents acted weird. She would be reassuring and encourage me to be forgiving.

I would sit in class all day thinking about her, looking forward to getting home after school. As soon as I got home I would call her.

It was always a disappointment if she wasn't home. Aunt Jess was deaf, so she wouldn't answer the phone. I'd worry about Aunt Mabel until I could get through to her. Then we'd laugh and joke and talk about the events of the day.

As I approached my twelfth birthday, I sensed that life was requiring something new from me. I didn't know what. I guess it was the beginning of a scary transition into adulthood.

I was in prep school. We were wearing jackets and ties everyday. I was looking a little too much like my father, who had clearly lost his way.

And when my father lost his way, my mother lost hers, careening out of control in his footsteps like a wagon whipsawed by a deranged horse.

But Mabel was steadfast, soft, and strong. She never wavered. She never lost her cool. She knew how to be firm and gentle, and wise.

When my parents asked how I'd like to spend my birthday, I suggested a party on Saturday with my schoolmates: hamburgers, hot dogs, ice cream, cake, and a funny movie.

But the night before, on the actual date of my birth, I wanted a quiet, candlelight dinner with Aunt Mabel and my family.

The truth is, I didn't really want my family there. I had no way of knowing what mood my alcoholic father might be in, whether or not he might create yet one more horrible, embarrassing scene.

Nevertheless, I wanted to try for some quiet "adult" time with Mabel before Saturday's party.

It was arranged. My love would be with me on Friday for dinner . . .

That afternoon, after school, I went to my mother's store in downtown Newark. I began calling Mabel, to tell her how excited I was that we would soon be together.

But there was no answer.

A little while later, there was still no answer.

And after an hour, two hours, three hours, there was still no answer.

I don't know why, but a sinister thought raced through my mind, stealing my life force like some fleet-footed demon.

"Wouldn't it be awful," I thought, "If Aunt Mabel was dead."

I pushed the despicable demon away.

I said to myself, "Stop having stupid, ugly thoughts!"

But it lingered.

I dialed her number again.

Still no answer.

Finally, our phone rang. My heart sang. "It must be Mabel!" I grabbed the receiver with glee.

It was our housekeeper, Maude. She sounded weird. "Johnny, put your mommy on the phone."

I handed the receiver to my mother.

She said, "Yes, Maude . . ." She listened. "Oh no!" she said, "When?"

"Yes, I guess I'll have to tell him."

My mother hung up the phone and sat frozen and still. There was a morbid, agonizing silence. I could see she was about to cry.

Finally, she turned to me. "Johnny, dear, I have some very sad news. Aunt Mabel won't be with us tonight, honey. Her son just called the house. She was hit by a car while she was crossing the street. I'm sorry, sweetie, she's dead."

The floor fell out from under me. I was in a desperate, headlong emotional free-fall, hurtling wildly through some dark, damp, cold abyss. There was no bottom to it. It was black, empty, and heartless.

I felt an explosion in my chest, like it had burst open, propelling my spirit out into some cold, dark corner of the Universe.

I cried.

I sobbed.

I wailed.

I was filled with jagged electric rage, despair, and disbelief. It was so cruel, so wrong, so sudden. This was my birthday! She was my love!

And suddenly . . . there was a cold, dark, stony, black hole of hard, motionless silence in that joyous space of light, love, and happiness that Aunt Mabel had brought into my life. It was chilling and numbing.

I pulled myself together. There was no birthday dinner that night.

But the next day I had fifteen friends coming to our house. My parents encouraged me to "be strong." After all, my friends expected a party, not a wake. My parents said, "Mabel would have wanted it that way."

So we went through the day making merry, having "fun," celebrating me. It was a profound lesson in turning away from sadness, in learning to deny what is real, in pushing away difficult feelings. It was all a little twisted and bizarre, because what I really wanted to be doing was healing my wounded heart.

But I played my part well. My friends never knew that my world had been shattered.

Two days later, at Aunt Mabel's funeral, I had an experience which helped me begin to perceive the tragedy in a much healthier way.

Walking into the funeral home, I was tense and frightened.

I was coming to see Aunt Mabel for the last time.

And I was surprised at how warm and comforting the atmosphere in the funeral home was.

We walked slowly and deliberately down the hall, as if we were about to encounter something dangerous.

We were guided into a room on the right.

There was a pungent smell of flowers in the air.

And there was Mabel, lying comfortably surrounded by the puffy satin lining of a soft grey casket. She was in a beautiful blue-grey dress, wearing her little-old-lady steel-rimmed glasses, her eyes shut peacefully. Her hands were folded across her stomach so sweetly and her gorgeous silver hair shimmered in the soft light.

She was wearing more make-up than normal. It gave her skin a soft, peachy glow.

And instead of the jolting shock of despair I had expected to feel, I sensed an ethereal warmth. It was as if, the moment I walked into the room, Mabel had reached out to hug me with two long, outstretched, spiritual arms.

As I walked to the side of her casket, I felt her arms around me holding me close to her. Inwardly, I felt her telling me, "It's all right, John dear. I'm fine. This is really not a tragedy. It was my time. I love you and I always will."

And what surprised me most was that this felt familiar. It didn't feel like I had been visited by some strange, ghostly being, or that anything really unusual had happened.

Rather, it was the sense that who she was, and who I loved, transcended the lifeless body that lay before me.

Our connection was real . . . it was heartfelt . . . it was eternal.

I knew that our love could never die . . .

And in that sense, Aunt Mabel could never die.

She would be with me always.

*I walked out of the funeral home on that cool late-autumn morning
with the sense that I was floating. There were no more tears, because I felt
Mabel with me, in my heart, now filling much more than that tall, graceful, elegant body that would soon be carried to the cemetery and buried.*

I felt her in the breeze, in the trees, in the sky . . .

But most of all, I felt her in my heart.

And since that day, more than thirty-five years ago, I always have.

There have been many times when I have missed her incredibly.

But I am so thankful for her love.

And I am thankful to her for teaching me that love can never die . . .

Many of us have experiences in childhood, or later in life, that
connect us to an inner place where we "know" that there is order in
the Universe, where we sense that what we perceive with our eyes,
our ears, and even our rational mind is not all there is to reality.

But, historically, our society has not been accepting of "non-sci-
entific" forms of experience and observation. We tend to discount
them either because they happened when we were children or
because some other force was at work. We assume that we were "out
of our head" be it with grief, intoxication, or joy.

Within a few months of my experience at Aunt Mabel's funeral I
had forgotten it.

But years later, when I began working with grieving and dying, it
came back to me. And only then, much later, did I really grasp its significance.

One of the most useful avenues to healing grief is the ability to re-
perceive and integrate the elements of our experience and our relationships that exist outside of what is measurable by science.

*If you have, even once in your life, experienced the bliss of love,
you know that the most joyous experience a human being can
have exists totally beyond the realm of reason and understanding.*

If we are to heal through our grief, we must be willing to experience our lives differently, to stop shutting off those glimpses of a deeper truth and a more profound reality. They are always with us, just beneath the surface of our awareness.

For most of us those glimpses have bubbled up into our awareness at a few critical moments in our lives. But like our scientific, materialistic culture, we have usually discounted them.

> *When we experience a profound loss, we often find that the devastating pain of grief completely undermines our view of the world and of reality.*
>
> *It not only tears open our hearts,* **it pries open our minds.**

In that state of openness, though we feel battered and bruised, we are often willing to explore the possibility that the way we have habitually looked at our lives and our world is no longer useful.

Our grief has shattered our Universe.

As we work to heal our grief, one of our tasks is to integrate that which we "see" with our eyes and that which we "feel" in our hearts. When we do that we have the opportunity to emerge from this experience living in a "larger" world — more wise, more loving, and *more fully alive.*

Chapter Five

HOW TO TURN LOSS INTO HEALING

The student gains by daily increment.
The Way is gained by daily loss.

CHAUNG TZU

THE WORD "WAY" IN THIS PHRASE IS ACTUALLY A TRANSLATION OF THE Chinese word "Tao."

"Tao" can be defined as the "way" to happiness . . . or the "way" to contentment . . . or the "way" to God.

It confronts us with a profound paradox: The suggestion that the "way" (to happiness) is gained by loss.

If so, the question arises, "What are we losing, and what are we gaining?"

To our rational western minds, it seems preposterous to suggest that loss is the route to happiness. But that appears to be exactly what Chaung Tzu is saying.

After all, we live in a society where it is assumed that happiness is achieved through the acquisition of material wealth and power and the development of fulfilling relationships.

And we clearly see that loss catapults us into great pain.

The easiest route to understanding Chaung Tzu's statement is to reflect on how many times in our lives difficulty has prompted growth. How often have we and our loved ones said, "That was the most awful experience of my life, but boy, oh boy, did I grow!"

When a loved one dies, a relationship ends, or a powerful desire is not fulfilled, we have lost something or someone external to ourselves. We think our life will forever be incomplete. We allow ourselves to believe that our inner happiness and our capacity to love are dependent on individuals and circumstances we have no ability to control.

The route through the sadness is to dive deeper into our own hearts, our own souls, our own intuitive trust.

Loss enters our life in a variety of ways. Some losses come suddenly, unexpectedly, with no opportunity to prepare, no ability to say good-bye, no chance to say what was left unsaid or to do what was left undone.

Others losses come over time, perhaps through a prolonged illness where the opportunities to "finish business" and "say good-bye" have been set against a backdrop of physical and emotional suffering; the body and sometimes the mind of a loved one slowly deteriorate until they are no longer suitable vehicles to hold the being we loved.

A relationship ends abruptly . . . or lingers on in a state of "near-death" for years.

Because our culture has, historically, given us precious little preparation for these inevitable experiences, at the moment a loved one dies or a relationship ends or we are told we're terminally ill, we often feel like we've crashed into a brick wall. We're confused and frustrated. We're shattered. We're dazed. We keep replaying the facts in our minds, desperately searching for some misunderstanding, some mistake, some missing piece that makes the reality turn out to be as unreal as we *feel* in our hearts it must be. The mind says, "This just simply couldn't have happened. I can't imagine my life without . . ."

And yet, when someone we love has died or has left us, each morning we wake and once again face the reality that they are physically gone. At times, we have to remind ourselves. It's as if we subconsciously hoped that the new dawn would bring a new reality . . . would rewrite history and erase the tragedy.

If we have lost a loved one through separation or divorce, we struggle to comprehend that which seems unthinkable, to expiate our horror that someone we loved has *chosen* to leave us. At times that is even more painful than dealing with their physical death.

In either case, there are moments when we feel their presence within us. We hear their voice. We smell their perfume. We see them vividly in our mind's eye. We can almost feel their touch. We feel the way we would if they were here.

But our intuitive, emotional sense of connection with them is at odds with our rational knowledge that they are gone. We are inclined to dismiss our sense of connection with them because we have no cultural context in which to understand it.

If we are working with a terminal disease in our own bodies, we have moments when we "forget" and, for whatever short period of time, we come out from under that dark cloud.

And if we sense that we may have participated in the onset of our disease, as we might with certain forms of cancer, heart disease, cirrhosis, or AIDS, we face the guilt and confusion of having lived our lives with ambivalence. We question why we consciously engaged in behaviors that might have hastened life's end.

Each day we make decisions about how to deal with these realities. We may approach the pain and the confusion a little bit at a time, step by step as the days go by, responding to some deep intuitive understanding that our ability to live life fully will either be enhanced or diminished by the degree of honest awareness we can bring to these events.

We may notice that our cultural training, which has been to ignore, deny, and avoid whatever is unpleasant, leads us deeper into confusion and numbness by offering only distraction as a solution.

We may also notice that the relentless effort of our mind to "understand" what has happened in some subtle way keeps the raw edge on our pain.

We are caught in the agonizing despair of our grief because we continually attempt to use our minds to resolve it, or to help us ignore it.

> *The real healing of grief can't take place until we make the journey from the mind to the heart. And when the heart is broken, the thought of reentering it is terrifying.*
>
> *But, the heart is precisely where the healing takes place. And when it is broken, it is also **wide open.***

For more than twenty years, I have made it a practice to visit with, to explore with, and at times care for people who are terminally ill. I also have spent a great deal of time intuitively navigating the sometimes stormy, sometimes fog-shrouded waters of grief—my own and that of many others.

Often in the course of social conversation when I tell people that I spend time sitting at the bedsides of people who are dying and holding the hands of people in grief, the response is one of shock bordering on horror. "Oh my God! How do you do that? That must be so depressing!"

At an earlier time in my life, I would have reacted the same way.

But at some point, because I had the opportunity to confront death so many times, I began to get the sense that in teaching us to avoid the unpleasant and encouraging us to deny and fight against the inevitable, our culture has robbed us of many, many precious opportunities to gain a deeper, more immediate sense of who we are and what our lives are all about.

We search desperately for meaning in life. We want to know that it all adds up to something, that we are not just random events in a trivial, uncaring, meaningless Universe. Intuitively, we sense that there must be something very profound about such an infinitely complex and intricate world.

But our cultural training encourages us to perceive the events of our lives and our world through a selective viewfinder. We always seek to filter out whatever is unpleasant.

And yet, here it is inside us. And there it is around us.

By diverting our eyes, our minds, and our awareness from so much of what exists in our environment, by pretending that aging, decay, danger, and death are best dealt with through avoidance and ignorance, we have short-circuited our ability to fully experience what it is to be human. At the same time we have cut off access to the parts of our beings that would be most helpful in times of emotional, spiritual, and existential crisis. We need only look at the widespread drug and alcohol abuse in our culture to realize that we are extremely unskilled at working with confusion, pain, and suffering. Most of us only know how to medicate and numb ourselves. We haven't got a clue about how to turn and face the demons that we think are tormenting us.

A number of years ago Ram Dass said to me, "If you want to get *really* high, try living in *Truth*."

For a long time I pondered the meaning of that statement. And slowly, primarily through the frequent interaction with grief and dying, I began to see that *Truth* has extraordinary power. That looking directly at *what is* is tremendously transformative. That every time we divert our eyes, every time we pretend that the people, places, and events of our lives are other than they are, we diminish our capacity to be *whole* beings. We subtly give ourselves the message that our hearts and minds are too small, too finite, too limited to handle the Universe and all of its infinite beauty and seemingly infinite horror.

So now I can share with you the certainty that dealing with grief and loss need not be depressing. In fact, it can be some of the most inspirational, uplifting, and meaningful work of a lifetime.

> *Death is our eternal companion . . . an immense amount of pettiness is dropped if your death makes a gesture to you, or if you just have the feeling that your companion is there watching you.*
> DON JUAN
> IN JOURNEY TO IXTLAN
> BY CARLOS CASTENEDA

When a loved one is ill or has died or we face a potentially terminal illness of our own, or we deal with divorce or separation, we are pushed beyond the boundaries our minds have created to maintain the illusion of safety, continuity, stability, and control. Our defenses crumble. We simply have no energy to support them.

We are thrust into an uncomfortable realm of confusion and apprehension. The ways in which we have known and experienced our lives, our loved ones, and ourselves are in disarray.

It is—amazingly enough—an extremely ripe moment. It is a time when we have the opportunity to break free of the prisons in our minds that have held us back from fully immersing ourselves in life. *It is a time to let go of pettiness and pretense.*

No, working with grief and dying does not have to be depressing. Of course, it can be *exhausting* if the care of a loved one involves demanding around-the-clock duties, little sleep, extraordinary effort to relieve suffering, meticulous attention to the minute details of medication, and on and on.

And it can be *difficult* if, no matter what is done, the loved one's condition continues to worsen or they and their family ride the roller-coaster of positive reports and improvement followed by negative reports and backsliding followed by more improvement followed by more worsening.

But it does not *have* to be depressing.

Working with grief and dying is *difficult* and *exhausting* when denial and aversion are present because *the psychological and emotion-*

al effort required to push away **Truth** *can completely sap the energy of every-one involved.*

> *It is not the illness, or the death, or the loss, or the grief that caus-es our suffering. It is our attempt to push it all away that caus-es our suffering.*

When we face it all openly and honestly, exploring the depths and subtleties of what loss, grief, and death have to teach us, the process can become profound. Sometimes it can even be humorous. At times, it even becomes joyous.

I do not mean to discount or trivialize the tremendous physical and emotional challenges that can be part and parcel of dying and loss.

But it doesn't *have* to be an unrelieved tragedy.

Over many years I have learned that even the greatest tragedies in life can become the groundwork for tremendous growth and insight. Profound loss can be the catalyst for the shedding of old skin, the loosening of rigidity. Profound loss can pave the way for a new alive-ness, a new enthusiasm, a totally new awareness.

I have seen dozens of people work with tragic and painful loss, with things so horrifying they seem completely unworkable. And slowly, eventually, many of those people come to a resolution of their feelings. In an astonishing number of cases, it's almost as if their life has been strangely enhanced by an experience they wouldn't have wished on their worst enemy. Would they choose not to have had the experience? In most cases, yes. But the fact is they did have it, and they made a decision to work with what the Universe put on their plate, no matter how distasteful it may have been.

> *If I were to briefly summarize what leads to a growthful resolu-tion of grief, I would say that instead of clinging to our models of how it should have been, or how we wish it was, we simply turn and look at life,* **as it is***.*

Religions and philosophical systems have struggled for centuries with the "question of evil." How can an all-powerful, all-knowing, all-loving, and all-good God create "evil?" How can bad things happen to good people? How can innocent people be "victimized" by evil people? How can we and our loved ones be so vulnerable?

We live in a physical Universe which operates according to certain basic laws. One of those laws is, "Every action has an equal and opposite reaction."

Taken literally, it means that the amount of "good" in the world must always be balanced by an equal amount of "bad," and vice versa.

It's a law.

The *road* to God, unity, peace, and happiness lies in doing what we consider "good" because "good" unifies.

And what we consider "evil" divides and separates.

So whenever we feel overwhelmed by the amount and ferocity of "evil" and negativity in modern society, we can take heart in the knowledge that *there is always an equal amount of "good."*

It's a law.

Religions and philosophical systems have done us a disservice if they suggest that being good and pious will protect us from difficulty, ill-health, problems, sadness, and death. They will not.

But we *have* been given *all* of the inner resources we need to deal effectively with *anything* that happens to us.

In the end, since the great problems and challenges of life are often the groundwork for the greatest growth, I don't feel qualified to judge what might be the highest grace the Universe can bestow, simply because, from my perspective, it looks painful or unfair or like something I wish you (or I) didn't have to go through.

I have come to understand that fighting against what happens to us in life only exacerbates our suffering. I have often seen people go through very positive transformations as a result of what I would categorize as suffering. So I am often at a loss as to what to hope for when I hope, or to pray for when I pray.

I just ask for the wisdom to work with whatever happens in life and to receive the unexpected as well as the expected with love, compassion, equanimity, and fascination. I want to deepen all my relationships. I want to open to the spontaneous joy in the Universe and to receive the spontaneous sadness with the awareness that the Truth *will* set us free. I want to know that being fully alive requires open awareness and a willingness to receive both joy and suffering as they present themselves.

> *To know that each day could be my last,*
> *or the last for someone I love . . .*
> *Helps me remember*
> *that there is no time to waste on*
> *pettiness.*

Chapter Six

BODIES ON THE BEACH

IT WAS THE SUMMER OF 1963 AND I WAS BEGINNING TO LOSE MY SENSE *of stability and security.*

After nearly twelve years of sobriety, my father had seriously committed himself to falling off the wagon. He was becoming extremely unpleasant to live with.

We were staying in a luxurious beachfront hotel in Puerto Rico. My father's company was having their annual convention and my father was engaged in some extraordinarily debauched behavior.

One morning he disappeared for several hours, showing up very drunk and very late for a 10:00 a.m. meeting he had scheduled in our suite. He told a long complicated story about having been in a taxi and desperately needing a bathroom.

He didn't explain why he was alone in a taxi in San Juan on a summer morning or where he was planning to go when he had a meeting scheduled back at the hotel. But no matter . . . He claimed that his efforts to explain his predicament to the Spanish-speaking driver resulted in his being delivered to a bordello.

And, oh, what a time he had there! What tribulations he experienced trying to explain to "the ladies" that he merely wanted a bathroom. The good old boys laughed, winked, and elbowed each other in the ribs before going on with their meeting.

My mother turned on her heels, went into their bedroom, and cried.

My father took no notice of her.

He said, "Hey, where are Fred and Don and Phil?"

"We don't know," said one of his lieutenants. "The last time we saw them was about four this morning. They were on their way out for a swim."

"Hope the poor bastards didn't drown," said my father, with all the concern of a hungry shark.

I left the room in disgust, went downstairs, and wandered out on to the beach.

It was about 11:30 a.m.

As I shuffled down the beach in a heartbroken stupor, my mind raged in confusion, desperately trying to understand what was so good about becoming an adult. Most of them seemed either drunk, or miserable, or both.

And what was it about alcohol that made them lose their emotional and moral bearings?

We were in an unfamiliar country. But everywhere I went those days felt unfamiliar.

I no longer knew my father.

And my mother was becoming encased in a victimized, punishing, isolated cocoon of sadness.

As I stumbled along the beach, I suddenly came upon a sight that stopped me dead in my tracks. Three lifeless bodies were sprawled out at the water's edge looking dead . . . or at least comatose.

I was gazing with astonishment at the supine bodies of Fred, Don, and Phil, my father's missing business compatriots. They had been dangerously, insanely, slobberingly drunk the night before and had decided to go for a midnight swim. When they staggered out of the surf in the pre-dawn hours, they passed out on the beach, sprawled like a big fat pod of dead whales.

Now, they were still unconscious, beginning to look like giant lobsters.
They had taken the full brunt of the Caribbean summer sun for five and
a half hours. They were dehydrated from the alcohol, unprotected by sun-
tan lotion, and completely numb and oblivious to the serious physical jeop-
ardy they were in.

Their skin was deep red, taut, and shiny. It was screaming. It was
alarming. It was disturbing. It had a too-late-for-hope quality. It was, lit-
erally, the color of a cooked lobster shell. I had never seen anything like it.

I thought they might be dead.

And although I sort of liked them, I thought they were stupid.

They had just been discovered by another fun-loving convention-goer
who was having trouble rousing them. He decided he should summon the
one medical doctor who was at the convention, if he could find the doctor
and if the doctor was sober enough to treat these three lunatics.

At that moment, I glanced up twelve stories and saw my mother stand-
ing on the enormous balcony of the presidential suite in which we were stay-
ing. She was waving her arms wildly, gesturing frantically, and shouting
something incomprehensible. She was clearly upset.

I assumed that she, too, had just discovered the carnage I was witness-
ing and had found it especially disturbing given the delicate emotional
state she was already in.

But as I looked up she seemed to be pointing to the huge stack of boul-
ders that punctuated the hotel's beachfront. I turned and looked. I couldn't
imagine what she was saying. The sound of the wind and the pounding
surf drowned out her voice. It was clear to me that the most urgent event
on the beach was the impending death of these three drunken fools. I ges-
tured toward them. She shook her head and frantically pointed toward the
rocks again, cupping her hands around her mouth and shouting some-
thing I still couldn't hear.

I turned toward the rocks, but still saw nothing unusual. Just loud
pounding waves and a noisy Caribbean wind.

I decided to go upstairs to find out what she was trying to communi-
cate. I went into the lobby, walked to the elevator, pressed the "up" but-
ton, and waited.

When the elevator finally descended to the lobby level, the doors opened and my mother came bursting out, tears streaming down her face, with my sobbing, hysterical sister following behind.

"My God!" I thought, "What has Dad done now?"

She was incredibly agitated and desperate. She grabbed me by the shoulders. "Where's Doctor Stephens?"

Ah, she wants the drunken doctor. Maybe, she's killed Dad. Oh no, that's too crazy. Maybe she, too, is concerned about the hungover, comatose lobster whales.

"I dunno. Dad's friends were just going to look for him."

My mother turned and started running toward the beach. "What about the boy? Did they see him?" she asked. She started running faster.

"What boy?" I started running to follow her.

"The boy that's stuck in the rocks."

"I don't know what you're talking about!" Now my mother, my sister, and I were all running as fast as we could, gasping for breath, bodies flushed with adrenaline.

We hit the sand. My mother frantically kicked off her high-heeled shoes and abandoned them so she could keep running. My sister and I did the same. The sand scorched our feet. My mother didn't seem to feel it.

As we approached the rocks at the edge of the surf, we saw the lifeguard now swimming against the pounding waves, struggling to get out beyond where they were breaking so he could approach the jagged boulders cautiously. He was trying to avoid being thrown against them by the relentless waves. Another lifeguard from an adjacent hotel came running across the beach and sprinted into the splashing white foam, diving under a wave to swim out to help his friend.

Then a third boy, perhaps fifteen or sixteen years old came running across the beach and also ran into the water, diving under the waves. Tears were running down his cheeks. He was screaming something in Spanish. He swam out to the others.

We watched the three young bodies bobbing in the waves, occasionally diving down under the surface, shouting words of assistance, encouragement, and warning to each other.

They seemed to be struggling to extricate something from the rocks. I was still a little confused.

"There's a boy stuck in the rocks. I think he's drowning," my mother sobbed.

A small crowd had now gathered. Doctor Stephens had been located . . . in the bar. He had stopped at his room to pick up his medical bag.

After a gruesomely long time and much indecipherable commotion, the three boys eventually emerged from the pounding waves dragging something . . .

*No . . . dragging some**one**.*

A boy.

Another boy.

A fourth boy. A younger boy. A younger boy with dark skin, short black hair, and a baggy, faded, yellow swimsuit.

His limbs were limp. Lifeless. His head hung like a wilted rose.

The two lifeguards were on either side of him. His back was toward us, his torso hung loosely. His head hung back over his upper torso and rocked back and forth like the pendulum of a clock. The lifeguards carried him by the arms, one on each side.

The third boy was following behind, struggling to get out of the water, now crying harder, wiping away tears and ocean water as he struggled against the erratic currents.

As they emerged from the shallow water, they hauled the fourth boy up the beach, dragging him so the backs of his legs made two wavy parallel tracks in the sand.

They dropped his arms. His body fell limp, heavy and still. I looked at the boy's face. His eyes were open. But he saw nothing.

The doctor looked stricken. He dropped to his knees and began artificial respiration. There was a somber air of futility about his efforts.

He pumped the boy's chest. Water poured from the mouth, but no breath.

He worked feverishly for about twenty minutes. The crowd stood silent, solemn, motionless.

Finally, Doctor Stephens stopped, heaved a great sigh, and sat back on his haunches.

He shook his head.

My mother sobbed. "Nobody saw him! I saw him from our balcony, but I couldn't do anything, and no one could hear me!" She was inconsolable. Her body shook in great spasms of despair. She had tried using the phone to communicate the emergency, but the Spanish-speaking hotel operator couldn't understand her hysterical ravings.

I thought I knew what I was witnessing, but it seemed inconceivable. "Is he dead?"

The question was a desperate grab for the handle of reality.

Doctor Stephens nodded.

I had so badly wanted him to say, "No. He'll be fine."

My heart froze. I felt its rhythm flutter, then stumble, then pound in my chest.

A cold chill ran through me.

An icy flush rose up my face.

I had never seen anyone die before.

Some conversation began on the beach. The third boy, the crying boy, was the dead boy's older brother. The dead boy was twelve.

I was twelve.

He lived nearby. He had been warned by his parents, his older brother, and the lifeguards not to swim near the rocks, but he didn't listen.

I had been warned by my parents not to swim near the rocks. I, too, sometimes didn't listen.

And in this small heap of salt-parched, sand-encrusted, lifeless flesh, we were witnessing the likely outcome of ignoring the warnings of wiser people.

But our hearts were too broken for blame.

The police arrived. The useless ambulance arrived. The boy was scooped up and carried off. His right arm fell from the stretcher and dangled loosely, his silent, thoughtless head turned toward me, his vacant, bloodshot eyes still open.

My mother continued to weep.

After a few stunned moments, one of my father's convention friends approached and said, "Doctor Stephens, can you come look at Fred and Don and Phil? I finally woke them up, but they're in pretty bad shape."

I had forgotten about them. And now, their predicament and its self-inflicted carelessness seemed a little ridiculous.

"Those damned idiots!" said Doctor Stephens as he got up off his knees, brushed the sand off himself, and looked in their direction. "And to think that they're still alive. This kid never had a chance."

With his shoulders slumped, Dr. Stephens, in his own hangover fog, wandered off to attend to the drunks.

They all had to go to the hospital. Two of them had to be admitted with third-degree burns. Morphine was prescribed for their pain.

And I stood frozen in a fog of existential confusion.

What opportunities had this boy missed?

The opportunity to "grow up?"

The opportunity to pollute his body with alcohol so that later he could risk death in other reckless ways? What was the dividing line between childhood and adulthood? . . . between immaturity and maturity? Just what chance was it that he never had?

I felt stunned, sad, nauseous, and shaken. I can still vividly see that boy's vacant, bloodshot eyes. I can still see those three dangerously sunburned drunks.

That day, for the first time, I saw someone my own age die. And I realized that if it could happen to him, it could happen to me.

And I saw my father's publicly announced excursion to the local bordello drive one more nail into the coffin of my parents' marriage.

And I saw three "grown" men whose insatiable craving for alcohol nearly caused them to die from over-exposure to the sun.

At first, the only people I really felt compassion for were the dead boy, the dead boy's family, and my mother.

But at some level, even then, I realized that Fred and Don and Phil were driven by some sinister disconnection from their inherent humanity, by some perverse inner demons that drove them to hurt themselves and their families just as my father was driven to hurt himself and his family. And I realized that their families could easily have gotten phone calls telling them that their husbands/fathers had washed up dead on the beach that day. They had escaped, for the time being, the fate the young Puerto Rican boy's family had to face.

But if they continued on the path they appeared to be on, their families might very well get that call someday.

So I felt compassion for all of them.

And my poor humiliated mother might have felt somehow perversely vindicated if it had been my father who drowned that day.

And so I felt compassion for her.

But what scared me the most was the realization that there was a part of me that envied the mysterious, vast, silent peace that the twelve-year-old boy had slipped into when he spent too much time underwater. At least he would no longer have to deal with what I was coming to know as the raging inconsistencies and hypocrisies of adulthood.

About five years later, Dr. Stephens, despite his conviction that Fred, Don, and Phil were "idiots," lost his medical license. He had taken to habitually prescribing narcotics for his friends whose only pain was existential confusion.

And Fred, who was the nephew of the company's owner, wound up as president and C.E.O. in 1968 when his uncle died from the complications of excessive alcohol and drug abuse.

The company, which had been extremely successful in the 1950's and 1960's, began to flounder. Tens of thousands of employees were laid off. Hundreds of retail outlets were closed. The product line failed to keep up with changing times and technologies. Fred couldn't be kept sober long enough to run a coherent executive meeting.

One day in 1980, Fred drank too much scotch and fell off the roof of his house. He sustained a devastating head injury that left him severely brain damaged.

I don't know what happened to Don and Phil.

But now I can reflect on all this with some degree of insight and compassion. That is a very precious gift the Universe has given me.

And although my life has been difficult at times, it has also been richly blessed.

That day, my father taught me that "having a good time" can be cruel if it is done without considering the feelings of the people who love you.

And Fred and Don and Phil taught me that just because we get older doesn't necessarily mean we become wiser.

They helped me to understand that happiness does not flow from abusing one's body. They taught me that there are natural laws that can not be violated.

I am eternally grateful to them for that.

But I am especially eternally grateful to that twelve year old boy. In giving up his life, he taught me to steer clear of many of the piles of dangerous rocks I have encountered since then.

As he drowned in the Ocean, I was drowning in confusion and sadness. I desperately wished he could have lived. Though we never met, and had never spoken, I felt an extraordinary kinship with him.

He taught me how fragile this life really is.

And he taught me that it can all change in the blink of an eye.

I never knew his name.

But I will never forget him.

*I only wish that . . . somehow . . . I could thank him . . . could thank his family . . . I wish I could tell him how grateful I am to him . . . I wish I could tell him how he opened my heart . . . I wish I could tell him that I have never forgotten him . . . I wish I could tell him that, somehow, I have tried to make the best of my life for **him**, as much as for myself.*

Chapter Seven

WHAT IS GRIEF?

"Grief is . . .
the impotent rage of being born
into a Universe of change."
CHARLES GARFIELD

EVERYONE HAS GRIEF. IT'S AN INESCAPABLE REALITY OF HUMAN EXIS-
tence.

We are not abnormal or weak because we experience grief. We
are merely touching the depths of the human experience, the chasm
between what we wanted . . . and what *is*.

From the first moment that we don't get exactly what we want
from the world, we experience grief. It may come as early as the
moment we leave the womb. Or it may come in the womb.

As infants we react with tears, sometimes in fear, sometimes in
pain, sometimes in rage. As we get older we learn to control our reactions. We become adept at concealing the tears, pain, and anger,

from ourselves and from others. But they are always there, lurking just beneath the surface.

And whenever we are faced with a cataclysmic loss in our lives, the accumulated grief of our entire lifetime rises to the surface.

At moments of profound loss, our defenses crumble. We no longer have the strength to stuff our feelings down. Sometimes just seeing another's tears is sufficient to trigger our own.

Many of us react to grief by distracting ourselves. Or we seek to gain economic, political, and social power to have the *illusion* of being able to control our internal and external environments. For many of us, when other distractions don't work, we numb ourselves with alcohol or drugs.

Our grief can be our undoing. It can turn us off to ourselves—to our lives and to our world.

Or . . . it can be the sword that tears our heart open, that allows us to be vulnerable, that takes away our illusion of control, our self-imposed distance from our capacity to love and surrender.

If we can meet our grief with courage and awareness, it can be the key that unlocks our hearts and forces us into a profound new experience of life and love.

In that sense, grief can be our friend . . . a fierce teacher, but a welcome wake-up call. It is the one thing that can jar us out of our propensity to sleepwalk through life and through relationships.

And what is "grief" other than the agonizing space of disharmony, disequilibrium, and discomfort between what we want from life and what we ultimately get? It is the vast reservoir of our accumulated past losses. It is the awareness of the inevitable losses to come. It is the sea of human disappointment.

It is the recognition that, ultimately, we have no control.

From our very first encounter with grief, our life has been a process of learning to cope with, to integrate, or to avoid the discomfort and disappointments we inevitably experience in life.

Many of us think of grief as the emotional pain surrounding the physical death of someone we love. But grief is much more complex, much more fundamental to our lives and the way we choose to live them.

At the very foundation of our society is the drive to avoid that which is unpleasant—to negate the aspects of life that would bring us disappointment. Instead of being taught how to deal with the inevitable disappointments and losses in our lives, we have been taught to ignore and deny them. We've been taught to "put on a happy face," "keep a stiff upper lip," and to "talk about something more pleasant." We want to "feel better fast." Many little boys have been taught not to cry because it's "unmanly." And many little girls have been taught that their emotions are irrational . . . an inconvenient byproduct of unbalanced female hormones.

Our entire culture is built on maximizing pleasure through the systematic avoidance of grief. We worship youth, beauty, strength, energy, vitality, health, prosperity, and power. We have confined illness, aging, and death to hospitals, nursing homes, funeral homes, and cemeteries. We treat these places like ghettos where distasteful things are happening and where most people in our society would rather not go unless they have to.

We spend billions of dollars each year on cosmetics, cosmetic surgery, hair transplants, hair dyes, liposuction, girdles, breast implants, breast reductions, genital enhancement, toupees, and wigs—all in an effort to change the ways in which our bodies don't measure up to the cultural model of "beauty." We don't want to look old, wrinkled, paunchy, or bald. The cultural model is so pervasive that we have evolved diseases like anorexia nervosa and bulimia. Their victims, mostly young women, would rather die of starvation than live with one ounce of fat on their bodies.

And when faced with a death, we hire "professionals"—funeral directors and cemeterians—who, historically, we have looked toward to help us keep grief at bay, to help us deny the reality and finality of

loss, the inevitability of change and decay. We don't want to participate in the process . . . we want to have someone else do it for us.

At every stage of our lives we are desperately trying to overcome
the ways in which our bodies and our world disappoint us. And yet,
the processes of aging and dying may have great lessons to teach us
about the natural order of the Universe and our place in it. We fail
to learn these lessons because we keep pushing them away.

A few years ago, when the accumulation of excessive material
wealth and possessions became a popular life goal and Donald
Trump was held up as a cultural hero, there was a popular bumper
sticker that read, "He who dies with the most toys wins!"

A more enlightened view might rather be, "He who dies with the
most *joy* wins."

And ironically, the road to joy lies not in avoiding the suffering,
sadness, and disappointment in life, but in learning to go through it,
to accept it . . . to grow in understanding, compassion, and love
because of it.

> *At the very same moment that we feel consumed by grief, we each
> have the source of all joy and happiness inside ourselves . . .*
>
> *Our grief is, in a very real sense, the mistaken belief that our
> happiness is connected to external things, situations, and peo-
> ple. It is the loss of awareness that happiness flows from within.*
>
> *So grief is more about the loss of connection to ourselves than it
> is about the loss of connection to a loved one or relationship.*

Even if we do remember that happiness flows from within, we feel
that something has happened which blocks our access to the source.
Our grief is largely the sadness of losing our connection to our inner-
most being . . . of feeling cut off from ourselves and therefore from
our ability to be happy. And no amount of monetary or material
accumulation can replace the connection with our "inner being."

In many societies which we have viewed as "primitive," *all of life* is
seen as a preparation for death. Every moment of uncertainty, every

surprise, every shock, every danger, every love, every relationship, every loss, every disappointment, every headcold—is seen as an opportunity to prepare for death, to learn to surrender to the inevitability of change, to acknowledge that life doesn't always give us what we want, to know with certainty that it can all change in the blink of an eye.

Our society has perceived life as an opportunity to deny the inevitability of aging, change, and death. And in so doing, we have robbed ourselves of the ability to feel connected to the natural way of things. We react to death and loss as "unfortunate," "incomprehensible," and "wrong."

But death just is. It is a fact of life. The way of *all* things is to arise, to take birth, to change, and ultimately to decay and die. Every living form in the physical Universe changes, decays, and dies. *Every* form.

The thought that our life should be other than it is at this moment, that the circumstances of our life, our family, our business, our world are unacceptable, is the groundwork of our grief.

Any thought that takes us out of *this* moment, whatever feelings and experiences *this* moment may hold, is the groundwork of our grief. The life and death issues in this Universe ultimately are beyond our control. We can be prudent, responsible, careful, and protective of our loved ones, but ultimately it is *all* beyond our control.

So grief is primarily the pain of resisting what is.

It is the inevitable outgrowth of our human mind thinking that the people, places, and events of our life should be *other than they are.*

It is also the sadness and despair of lost opportunities. I notice in myself a grief about the passing of my own youth, a sadness that one day, inevitably, each of my loved ones and I will part for the last time. And in each relationship I've lost, whether through death or some other form of parting, I experience a frustration about the opportunities that were missed—about the ways in which two hearts stayed separate, the frustration over our failure to become one, the ways in which I/we could have been more, done more, said more, given more.

This book is about the ways in which our society has sought to avoid grief. It's about the ways in which that avoidance has prevented us from being fully human. It's about the methods we can use to begin to deal effectively with the grief in our lives.

Ultimately, it's about *happiness* . . . the happiness that arises within us when we begin to have space in our hearts to handle life in its totality. The joy, the love, the fun—and the frustration, sadness, and anger. It's all workable.

The process of opening our hearts to all of it
is the process of healing grief.

Chapter Eight

MY MOTHER'S EYES

IN 1967 AT THE AGE OF 54 MY MOTHER HAD A LARGE CANCEROUS SEC-*tion of her colon removed and in late 1968 she was diagnosed with a fast-growing, malignant brain tumor. I was seventeen. My father sought out the finest internists, surgeons, and oncologists in the world. His wife, he said, would have nothing less than the best medical care money could buy. But the verdict was unanimous—there was nothing to be done.*

Nevertheless, her medical team recommended a series of excruciatingly painful experimental tests and devastating chemotherapy treatments which made my mother violently ill, completely sapped her strength, and left her despondent, demoralized, psychologically defeated, and completely bald.

But no one considered discussing her condition openly and honestly. Nor was she consulted about her treatments. She wasn't told about the negative side effects of the treatments nor was she given an opportunity to make any decisions about her treatment. Telling someone who was terminally ill that they were dying was thought to be cruel. It was a complete social taboo.

It was further assumed that a dying person and to some extent their family was incapable of making any informed, rational choices about the medical procedures to be followed. At every step along the way the patient was an unwitting participant in a process that unfolded in mysterious, often painful daily surprises. The participation of the family was limited to giving a "yes" or "no" answer to what was, on the part of the doctors, essentially a rhetorical question. "Do you want us to do everything possible to save your mother (even though we have already told you that it's hopeless)?" "Yes," was the assumed, expected, and universally delivered answer.

Once the doctors were given the "go-ahead" no further questions were asked nor were any explanations given. It was assumed that the medical issues were too complicated to be discussed and the emotional issues were too painful to be discussed. The process of frantic, futile treatment lumbered on like a roaring, directionless old steam engine with no discernible destination, ultimately reaching the end of the tracks and falling on its side . . . or crashing inevitably into a stone wall.

After a number of weeks in the hospital, my mother's medical team announced that there was nothing further they could do. It was suggested that she be removed to a nursing home where she would continue her downward slide into oblivion.

When my mother was informed of the plan, she protested. She didn't want to go to some unfamiliar nursing home. She wanted to go home. She discussed the possibilities with our family doctor.

*He listened patiently to her pleadings and then took the rest of the family out into the hall. He spoke with sadness and resignation. "I understand her feelings. We could have a hospital bed set up at home and we could arrange for around-the-clock nursing care. But you don't want **that** in your house. **That's** a real mess."*

*"**That** mess" he was referring to was the process of dying.*

But we did eventually bring her into our home. It was frightening, because we had no idea what would happen to her or how it would affect us.

For several weeks we watched her and sat with her as she slowly, gently, naturally, and peacefully slipped away, content that she was surrounded by her family, in her own home, reassured by the love we all shared and silently acknowledging the confusion we all shared.

We didn't have the skills we now have to deal with dying and grief. We had to rely on our intuition. And we had to find some trust in the Universe.

But I was a depressed adolescent. I had lost my trust in the Universe. Ironically, it was my mother's death which drew that trust out of me again. During those weeks I experienced something deep inside me, something beyond my intellect, that felt very peaceful about it all. When I stood back from my fear, her dying began to feel like a natural process.

Years later, I heard someone say, "Dying is absolutely safe." And that is what I instinctively felt during those weeks with my mother. Her body was changing and falling away. I don't know why, but somehow I felt that she was safe.

She ultimately lost the ability to speak. Our house became very quiet as the rest of us spoke in soft, hushed tones. It almost took on the atmosphere of a temple, or shrine, or holy place. There was an overwhelming sense of awe, as if she was preparing to go on a great exploration or voyage. In the spring of 1969 as our country was preparing to journey to the Moon, my mother was preparing to go beyond.

She and her hospital bed and medications had moved into the guest room. There were nurses on duty around the clock. I sometimes avoided going in to see her, because I didn't know what to say. The trivial, contrived small talk we often fall into at such times now seemed profane. I gagged on the very thought of meaningless chatter in the face of the most awesome event I had ever witnessed.

One afternoon I walked in and sat on the edge of her bed. My mother had been an elegant, glamorous woman. But now she looked hideous— bald from the ravages of chemotherapy, except for a few remaining wispy, ragged strands of her soft platinum hair. Her head seemed huge, ghostly pale, and uncommonly round. Her right eye was swollen and protruding from its socket. She looked like something from a horror movie. It was excruciating to look at her.

But she seemed so peaceful . . .

She lay silent and looked at me. I looked at her. I took her hand in mine. She had no energy left, but I felt her squeeze my hand so subtly . . . so tenderly. I looked deep into her crystal blue eyes.

I kept looking and as I looked her eyes got deeper and deeper and deeper. Our eyes locked, and for the next thirty minutes we never diverted our gaze away from each other. We just sat there gazing. And I looked back and back and back . . . deeper and deeper into her soul.

Her hideously deformed body began to fade away. And I looked deeper and deeper and deeper. It was like riding through a tunnel to the core of her soul.

And suddenly, deep within that withered hulk of a body, was the being I knew as my mother. Her love, her care, her nurturing, her compassion, all shone through more radiant than I had ever seen them before.

All the barriers between us melted away in the brilliance of the light within her. I sensed that as her body withered, her soul had gained strength.

She squeezed my hand again. And as she did, she gently nodded her head two or three times. In that moment, though not a word had passed between us, I knew that we had said everything that needed to be said. It was okay. She was okay. We loved each other deeply. We honored each other completely. And we were grateful for the love we had shared all these years. She would go on and I would go on, and the place we had touched together would never disappear for either of us. Because somehow, in her room that day, my mother and I had shared a glimpse of eternity.

I felt tears, but they were tears of awe and gratitude more than sadness. And I knew that because I had been willing to go past my horror and fear, to look past her physical deformities and look deeply into her soul, that I had seen her more clearly and contacted her more intimately than ever before.

A few days later she died. It was a beautiful, peaceful Sunday afternoon. A glorious sunset washed our house in brilliant golden hues, and a warm, gentle breeze soothed and caressed us. A profound aura of peace filled our home. My father, my two sisters, and I all held hands around my mother's bed and kissed her good-bye. Then my father, my two sisters, and I put our arms around each other and, probably for the first time ever, shared a family embrace. We put our heads together and all softly cried.

After a while, we silently moved outdoors. The sun had nearly set, but not quite. As I looked at it, something occurred to me that I had never noticed before: The sun is most radiant when it's setting. And though it disappears from view, it never dies.

I felt the same about my mother. Like the sun, she had faded from view. But I knew she'd always be with me, even in the darkest hours.

I looked at my family and marveled at the sense of closeness and intimacy we all felt, at how this moment of wonder and sadness had melted away all the walls of separation families usually hide behind. For that moment, the resentments, petty anger, and judgments dissolved into the familial love we all shared. We were one consciousness . . . one heart. My mother, in giving up her own life, had finally brought the rest of the family together in a closeness and bond that we share to this day. Simultaneously we felt profound sadness and profound joy.

Her death, in our home, was not a mess.

It was her final blessing.

And so, thanks to my mother's insistence that we not surrender to the fearful preconceptions and rigid notions of the medical establishment, I had the opportunity to watch the process of death for the first time in my life. The experience was absolutely life-changing.

At her funeral, my high school friends marveled at how well I was handling my grief. Several of them expressed the conviction that if one of their parents died they would be devastated to the point of incapacity.

But I knew something they couldn't know, and it seemed so peculiar within the context of our societal horror about death that it was difficult for me to express. Prior to my mother's death I had been a confused, desperate, and depressed adolescent. I was seeing a psychoanalyst twice a week. Now my mother had died and I felt peaceful about it.

When I conveyed my feelings to my psychiatrist, his response was, *"It took a lot of courage for you to tell me that."* That was all he had to say. And although he, too, was a highly skilled and profoundly insightful member of the medical community, he had responded with a certain lack of wisdom and compassion when I had first told him that my mother was terminally ill. He said, *"Don't worry. What we do with people who are dying is to get them addicted to narcotics. Then they're quiet and they aren't a problem. Your mother won't be a problem."* What was most amazing was that he delivered this message with a tone of warmth and concern. He was trying to alleviate my sadness and anxiety.

In the twisted milieu of our society's aversion to that which is unpleasant, this fine doctor, like many others, had mistaken coldness and callousness for compassion.

Chapter Nine

WHY ARE WE THIS WAY?

You are frightened of death
because you have postponed it.

J. KRISHNAMURTI
IN *FREEDOM FROM THE KNOWN*

IN THIS REMARKABLE STATEMENT, THE GREAT PHILOSOPHER, Krishnamurti, has summarized the essential problem with our culture's approach to death and loss. We are frightened of it because we have "postponed" it.

In his wonderful book, *Freedom From The Known*, Krishnamurti says further:

> *"You cannot be frightened of the unknown because you do not know what the unknown is . . . Thought, which breeds the fear of death, says, 'Let's postpone it, let's avoid it, keep it as far away as possible, let's not think about it'—but you are thinking about it. When you say, 'I won't think about it,' you have already thought out how to avoid it . . . Most of us are frightened of*

dying because we don't know what it means to live. We don't know how to live, therefore we don't know how to die. As long as we are frightened of life we shall be frightened of death."

So how do we stop postponing death?

HISTORICAL AND CULTURAL PERSPECTIVES

Over the past fifty years our culture has evolved through extraordinary changes in nearly every aspect of our family, professional, and social lives, and the pace of these changes keeps quickening. Superficially, we see the realization of the technological dreams of decades past. We are living in the world of the future. Our world and our homes are filled with amazing gadgets, remarkable instruments of communication, unbelievable modes of transportation, and seemingly limitless access to information. If we could turn our perception backwards to see the world of 2000 through the eyes we had in 1950, we might think we were living in a science fiction movie.

Alongside this incomprehensible stream of technological advancement has come a great deal of social upheaval and philosophical turmoil as we struggle to grasp the meaning of human life, both individually and collectively, in a world dominated by machinery and invention. We have begun to recognize that much of what we strove to accomplish technologically in an effort to improve human life has actually created new problems. We have come to recognize that technology is expensive. It carries not just economic costs, but unforeseen costs to nature, the environment, and to the psychological and spiritual lives of human beings.

The tension between unbridled technology and the psycho-spiritual side of humanity has manifested itself in countless ways. The one that is particularly germane to our discussion is the evolution that has taken place over the past thirty years in our thought and practice regarding mortality and death.

As a child growing up in the 1950's and 1960's, I absorbed a worship of science, technology, and the human intellect that was nearly absolute. Not only would our intellects take us to the moon and beyond, we thought that medical science might even, one day, find a cure for death. Little by little we would gradually develop a vaccine and/or a cure for every major disease including cancer and heart disease.

In the 1970's, we saw the birth of cryogenics, a new method of freezing human bodies immediately following physical death. The assumption was that later, when the cure for death or for that person's cause of death, was found, the body could be unfrozen and brought back to life. Cryogenics was and is very expensive, and is therefore only accessible to a small number of human beings. But it demonstrates the extreme attachment to form and the extraordinary devotion to science that has permeated our entire culture.

We have believed that new surgical procedures would be found to correct all the inconveniences and aesthetic disappointments of the aging process. We have believed that emergency medicine would evolve procedures to resuscitate accident victims, heart attack victims, and other patients with acute trauma. Miraculous medical healings would become commonplace.

And medical science *has* made incredible strides. Average life expectancy has increased dramatically. But human beings still die. New, virulent, unrecognizable diseases spring up every day, some of which are brought on as byproducts of technological advancement. It's as if there is an inescapable law governing humankind demanding that our relationship with nature not be one of domination, but of cooperation and harmony. It's clear that many of the avenues we have taken during the twentieth century have taught us that there are certain inviolable natural laws which don't take kindly to our arrogance.

THE BEGINNINGS OF CHANGE

During all of the social upheaval of the 1960's a new perception of death began to emerge in our culture. Like many of the social changes brought on during that decade, it began as a fringe movement. It is now so fully dispersed throughout the society that we barely notice the dramatic changes that have taken place as a result.

We began to realize that technology could not and would not solve all human problems, nor could it create immortality. We began to realize that our fixation on technology was causing us to treat human beings as machines. We began to realize that a deleterious one-dimensionality had developed in our perception of humanity and that humanity was suffering greatly because we were failing to recognize the totality of our interconnection with nature and with the spiritual essence at the core of our beings.

The destructive aspect of this skewed perception was most noticeable in what has been described as our cultural denial of death. British author Jessica Mitford poked fun at us in her book *The American Way of Death* which examined what she perceived as the peculiar beliefs and practices of a culture that had lost its connection with the natural order of the Universe.

But more to the heart of the matter is the movement that began in the 1960's which now manifests itself in a profusion of both inpatient and outpatient hospice groups, grief therapists and grief therapy groups, cancer patient support groups, and groups for family members of cancer patients. Hundreds of different kinds of support services, workshops, and seminars are now available for people who are terminally ill and their families. Living wills are becoming commonplace. Many colleges, universities, and high schools offer courses on "Death and Dying" and they are often extremely popular and heavily enrolled. Funeral homes and cemeteries are sponsoring bereavement groups as part of their community outreach and service to families. More and more are training their staff members in communicating effectively, with greater sensitivity toward the grieving families they serve.

And the medical community has been forced to begin treating patients as "whole" beings who have a right to know the full extent of their condition and to participate in decisions about their treatment. As a culture, we have begun to recognize that we unfairly patronize people when we adopt the view that we know what is "best" for them. "Empowerment," a popular word in our lexicon these days, suggests that at every level an individual should be "empowered" by having access to the information and tools of decision-making that enable them to run their own lives, as they see fit, up until the moment they die. While this shift in consciousness has been a difficult pill for the medical community to swallow, great progress has been made. The atmosphere in many hospitals is distinctly different from what it was thirty years ago.

But, interestingly enough, although the size and scope of technological advances has been extraordinary, the most profound changes have come in the manner in which patients and their families are treated and the manner in which they are becoming a more integral part of the process of healing and/or easing the way for a more gentle death. Most people now have a negative perception of "extraordinary measures" taken to keep a body breathing and a heart beating once the "quality of life" is gone.

While the overall impact of this shift may be difficult to assess for years to come, it is undoubtedly significant. It would appear that our society is ready to begin unwinding the grip of fear and denial that has traditionally surrounded aging, death, and loss.

We have seen dramatic changes in the manner in which people seek to deal with the logistics and rituals of burial and memorialization. Cremation, once thought of as religiously, psychologically, and aesthetically abhorrent, has gained a significant level of acceptance. Each year the number of people choosing cremation over traditional ground burial and/or mausoleum entombment rises dramatically. And the number of people choosing new and different forms of funeral service continues to rise. These new forms often engage and involve family members and friends much more than has been common in decades past.

Many innovative, genuinely caring funeral directors are seeing themselves in a changing role, and are learning new ways of providing meaningful, healing services for the families that come to them.

More and more funerals are becoming a unique "celebration of life" for the deceased rather than a dramatic and maudlin period of mourning and despair orchestrated in a "cookie-cutter" format.

And funeral "pre-planning" is becoming more and more common. Within the context of our culture, it's the most effective way I know to stop "postponing" death. Other, more "primitive" cultures often give adolescents, as they pass into adulthood, some symbol that acts as a daily reminder of their mortality. They don't want their young to learn how to "sleepwalk" through life. They want their children to share the aliveness that comes from knowing each day might be their last.

But our culture has no such device. We have tried to remove all reminders of our mortality, and all reminders of how fragile our lives really are.

The one "ritual" we do have which can function as a welcome wake-up call is pre-planning our funerals. The practice of sitting down with one's spouse, or one's family, discussing and making the arrangements with a funeral director and/or cemetery for the disposition of one's body when one dies, can bring an amazing new aliveness to a marriage and to family relations. It may provide the first real opportunity for a couple to look in each other's eyes and consciously acknowledge that they will not be together forever . . . that there is no time to waste on pettiness.

Of course, many people are filled with superstition and fear that if they pre-purchase a casket and cemetery property, or pre-arrange a cremation, they will use these things sooner than they might have.

But that's just more fear.

Eventually, they *will* use them. The real question is, how much of their time on earth will they use? Arranging one's own funeral can be an excellent way to remind ourselves, and our loved ones, to use every moment of this precious life.

These changes in our culture are, for the most part, extremely healthy and represent our desire to engage the truths, realities, inevitabilities, and natural law of the physical Universe much more

fully and consciously than has previously been the case in western civ-
ilization. As we progress technologically, we realize that there must
be a concomitant progression of development of the human spirit.
Technology can only satisfy one level of our multi-dimensional
beings. We are learning to use its limitations as a jumping-off point
for our emotional, spiritual, and psychological development.

The work we are talking about here is at once totally joyous and
incredibly difficult. It is the work of opening fully to our humanity
and to our spirituality and gaining some insight into their relationship. It is the work of stopping the pushing away of the inevitable and
learning to live more fully in the face of it. It is the work of recognizing that every day might be our last or the last for our loved ones.
We therefore must begin to prioritize our lives in the face of that
recognition so that each day we are *fully alive, fully engaged,* and *fully
loving.*

In a number of monastic spiritual traditions throughout the
world monks are instructed to spend time in cemeteries reflecting
on the ultimate end of all life in form and meditating on the Eternal
Truth or Spirit that lies beyond form.

Most of us want to divert our eyes when we pass a cemetery . . . we
enter reluctantly, when we have to, with a psychic shield over our
heads and around our eyes, afraid to look or to touch anything as
if death might be catching. We leave with a sigh of relief, secure in
the knowledge that, today at least, we were able to leave the cemetery . . . upright and conscious.

Imagine that we, too, like the monks, might spend time in a cemetery reflecting on the profound existential truths that exist there.
Each time we pass a cemetery, a funeral home, or a funeral proces-
sion we might take a moment to reflect on the grieving families that
live out these rituals every day. *What can they teach us about seizing the
moment, loving our families, and stopping the postponement of our lives?*

In point of fact, those of us who spend time with people who are
dying and/or grieving can learn many great and profound lessons.
We learn that our fear of death is directly equitable with our fear of

life. Not only is it equatible, it's exactly the same fear. It's the fear of the unknown. It's the fear of the loss of control. It's the fear of what may be around the next corner. It's the fear of incompleteness and disappointment. To the extent that we fear death we will also fear life, and vice-versa. We learn what many, many spiritual traditions and nature-based cultures have long sought to teach us— that we can't ever be *fully alive* until we consciously recognize that we will die someday, and we don't have any guarantees about when that day will come.

While the actuaries tell us that we have 70+ years to live, I have seen an awful lot of people die well before that age from a million different unpredictable causes. Haven't you?

In this world of form
the only things that are guaranteed
are change and death.
Beyond that we have no guarantees.

Chapter Ten

BRINGING DEATH OUT
OF THE CLOSET

My dying patients taught me so much more than what it was like to be dying. They shared lessons about what they could have done, and what they should have done, and what they didn't do until it was too late, until they were too sick or too weak, until they were widowers or widows. They looked back on their lives and taught me all of the things that were really meaningful, not about dying . . . but about living.

ELISABETH KUBLER-ROSS
IN *THE WHEEL OF LIFE*

IN 1966 A SWISS-BORN PSYCHIATRIST NAMED DR. ELISABETH KUBLER-Ross embarked on a journey that has spanned four decades and set in motion a process that has dramatically altered the way Americans perceive death.

As a professor in the Department of Psychiatry of the University of Chicago Medical School, Dr. Ross suggested to her medical and seminary students that an exploration of the psychological dynamics of people with terminal illnesses would be a useful learning experience. What feelings and emotions do people who are dying experience? How do they cope with their situation? What is helpful to them as they try to make sense of the most profound and awesome life transition they have ever experienced? How do they deal with the existential dilemma posed by the inevitable end of every human life?

A number of Dr. Ross' students quickly became enthusiastic about the project. She offered to accompany them to Billings Hospital at the University of Chicago where she would facilitate their meetings with patients who had been given terminal diagnoses in order to identify potential interview subjects.

But when she took her students to the hospital, they were confronted by a most unexpected and amazing surprise: There was no one dying in the hospital!

At least that's what the nursing staff wanted them to believe.

Every head nurse on every ward at Billings expressed shock and outrage at the suggestion that dying patients be interviewed. Then they denied that there were any on their ward. Dr. Ross heard all this, went back to her office, leaned back in her chair, closed her eyes, and said, "I think Americans have a problem with death."

Ironically, it took this diminutive Swiss-born woman doctor to point out to us that this absolute inability for anyone in the medical community to accept, acknowledge, and work with the natural and inevitable process of dying represented a fundamental core sickness in our culture. In modern America we have been taught to worship youth, beauty, vitality, strength, wealth, and health. Old age, sickness, and dying have been shunned and treated as vulgarities. The deification of science and technology has led us to believe that inevitably they could overcome all problems, negativity, suffering, and inconvenience in human life; that finally, medical science might even find a cure for death. In the meantime, it was as if people who died were treated as unfortunate victims of a research process that was taking too long. The medical community reacted with disdain to those who dared to signal a failure of the research process by dying before a cure was found.

Psychiatrist R. D. Laing said, *"Life . . . is a sexually transmitted disease that is always fatal."* For Laing, there was humor and irony in his statement. But for most of the mid-twentieth century medical community, prior to Elisabeth Kubler-Ross' seminal work in the field, every fatality was a demonstration of the failure of their work.

But Elizabeth pointed out to the medical community and then to our society at large that no matter how extraordinary the tools and measures available to doctors may be, eventually, inevitably, *everyone must die.* If that is the given and inescapable end of all human life, no matter what doctors do, then perhaps we would be healthier as a society if we would embrace the inevitable rather than pushing against it. Perhaps we should begin to recognize that, as Ecclesiastes points out, there is "A time to be born and a time to die." It is even conceivable that there is a time when a human being is ready to die, not from a depressed or suicidal perspective, but from a deep intuitive recognition that their work on earth is finished. In any event, since everyone does inevitably die, perhaps the most compassionate act is to help them and to help their loved ones prepare, to help them "finish business," to allow for the opportunity to resolve that which remains unresolved and to do (to the extent possible) whatever they sense remains undone in their lives.

As with anyone who questions an ingrained social paradigm, Elisabeth ran into fierce opposition in the early years of her work. Her response to the stonewalling nurses who denied that there was anyone dying on their wards was to take her students by the hand and boldly march them past the nurses' stations using her trained medical eyes to search from room to room for patients who clearly were nearing the end of their term on this earth.

When she saw someone who looked like a candidate, she would gently move into their room, stand at their bedside, and introduce herself. "I'm Dr. Ross," she would say, "and this is my student so-and-so. We're going around the hospital visiting with patients today. What's happening with you?"

Interestingly, the openness of her question often led to a surprising answer like, "I'm full of cancer and no one will talk to me about it. They all pretend it's not happening. I've never felt more alone in my life."

Then Elisabeth would ask, "Would you like to talk about it?" and the answer was often a desperate, "Yes. Please."

In those early years she learned many profound lessons. One of the most important came when she conducted a preliminary interview with a patient who said, rather urgently, "Dr. Ross, I need to talk to you right now!" It happened that Elisabeth had another commitment and she promised to come back the next day.

But the next day when she came back to visit, she discovered that the patient was now too sick to talk. He died later that same day.

A precious opportunity had been lost. But before this patient died, he said to Elisabeth, "Dr. Ross, Thank you for trying."

In a world of such uncertainty
there is an inherent danger in postponement.

Chapter Eleven

THE RAGING FIRE THAT IS OUR GRIEF

THE TWO FUNDAMENTAL MIND-STATES THAT SEEM TO UNDERLIE ALL grief and difficult loss are:

1. A PROFOUND SENSE OF INCOMPLETENESS

and

2. DEEP SADNESS OVER LOST OPPORTUNITIES.

When a relationship ends, through death, divorce, or any other form of separation, our first reaction is panic and disbelief. The pain of our hearts breaking is so excruciating that our minds have no way to contain the chaotic onrush of thoughts and emotions. We scream, we rage, we cry, we pace up and down. Our minds feel like their very substance is unraveling. Our skin crawls. Our body feels like a prison. Our stomach hurts. Our chest tightens. We're tortured . . . terrified. Our thoughts race in frantic, irrational, spiraling patterns. We bounce back and forth between desperate disbelief and terrifying certainty. The onrush of "what if's" begins. We seek some way to blame ourselves. What could we have done differently? What could our loved one have done differently? What could the medical community have done differently? Why didn't the therapist see this coming? Why wasn't I there? Why didn't they give him better care? Why weren't they more attentive?

If only he hadn't bought that fast car . . . if only I had been there . . . if only her diet had been different . . . if only he had gotten more exercise . . . if only he had never met that awful woman who . . . if only he had worn a condom . . . if only she had never touched that first glass of scotch . . . that first narcotic. If only he hadn't gone there . . . if only *I* had been there. If only the doctor had acted sooner . . . if only *I* had recognized the signs sooner.

The heart finds no refuge in the mind; the mind finds no comfort in the shattered heart.

Why did this have to happen now? How will I go on? Why should I go on? I can't take this pain. I don't want to live. I can't live without him. I don't want to live without her. My life will never be happy again. We never got to take that trip to Europe . . . Couldn't we have had one last dinner at . . . ? Why didn't I ever tell her that I . . . ? Why couldn't he ever take responsibility for . . . ?

We lie awake at night tormented by our thoughts of injustice and our sense of self-hatred, replaying the events over and over again trying to re-program a different, more satisfying, ending. The sunrise brings only modest respite from the dark, terrifying despair. We're exhausted. But the mind won't stop racing. It's never been stronger, more willful. It insists on searching for a way out, a happy ending. And it insists on placing blame somewhere, on something, on someone—mainly on ourselves.

Ultimately, we become depleted. And our panic turns to numbness. If we can't find that numbness on our own, we will drink or take drugs or ask our doctor to prescribe something to deaden the pain of our human existence.

From within the numbness we look out on our lives with dispassion and disinterest. We've found a way not to care. We stumble around in a daze, only partially alive, but temporarily free of the agonizing pain of resisting change and loss.

And yet, somewhere inside we know that the habitual attempt to anesthetize ourselves into numbness only diminishes us further. That a large part of our grief is the sense of lost opportunity, and that most of the lost opportunities occurred while we were with our now missing loved one. At some level, our grief is not always about their lack of presence in our life now—*it's often about our lack of presence in their life when we **were** with them.*

LAURA AND TED

When Laura married Ted, he was already well beyond being HIV positive and had moved into active AIDS. He was very sick and had been through many devastating and debilitating treatments.

Laura and Ted shared a profound love and had been friends for years. They married, in spite of his illness, to honor and complete the deep commitment they had made to each other.

Their love and devotion led to increased efforts toward healing. And, in one of the most extraordinary healings I have ever witnessed, Ted retreated from the brink of death in an absolutely incomprehensible manner.

He had been sick for several years during which time Stephen and Ondrea Levine and I had all been working with him and with Laura.

Finally, in November of 1995, Laura called me to say that Ted was in St. Vincent's Hospital in New York and that the doctors had advised her that, at best, he had about two days to live. She asked if I would come into the city to see him. I went the next day.

He was essentially comatose, sallow and unresponsive, his eyes rolled up in their sockets, his breath shallow and irregular. His hair was flat and matted from days of high fever and constant sweats. His skin had that sticky, clammy, translucent quality people get just before dying.

By that time I had been with many people just prior to their deaths. Based on what I saw, I wouldn't have been surprised if Ted had died while I was there in his room. He seemed just hours, if not minutes, from dying.

I spent about an hour with him and then spent some time in an adjacent room with Laura. When I left, I expected to get a call, in at most a few days, telling me that Ted had died.

But the call never came. For some mysterious, miraculous reason, Ted slowly began to improve and wound up living another three years.

It created an interesting predicament for Laura. Her tenure as caregiver lasted much longer than she had anticipated. It was an extremely complicated, time-consuming, and demanding process. Ted was a joyous, angelic being caught in a fragile, weakened body. His post-coma mind was not always tuned to the channels the rest of us are usually on.

And he could be difficult. Sometimes he would angrily demand all kinds of unreasonable things. At other times he would sob uncontrollably for long periods, expressing an unnamed, unknowable, profound grief.

Once, in the middle of a bitterly cold winter, he snuck out of their apartment and wandered off barefoot and coatless down Seventh Avenue in New York City in search of exotic, totally inappropriate foods that would have disrupted his very delicate nutritional regimen. He got lost and confused, jeopardizing his already precarious health, inviting back the pneumonia that had almost killed him previously.

Keeping his medications and nutrition in balance was a full-time, frustrating, ultimately futile endeavor.

But Laura persisted. At times she came close to burning out. At times the frustration and tension were so great for her that she could barely sit in the same room with Ted.

But her love for Ted, and his love for her, sustained her. For the most part, she saw her role as a divine gift, one she was grateful to fulfill impeccably. It took extraordinary amounts of time, energy, and patience, but Laura always seemed to be able to draw on some amazing, mystical source of renewed strength every time she was near the end of her rope.

Since Ted had survived some incredibly close encounters with death, many of those around him began to perceive him as invincible. When his death finally came, a full three years after the doctors had pronounced his comatose body just hours from dying, it was a shock to many of those around him, most notably Laura.

She told me that his passing was "Beautiful . . . incredibly peaceful."
She held two memorial services for him which were "inspirational."

But a couple of weeks later, when the emptiness of the household began
to set in and she was surrounded with constant reminders of his life and
now his absence, her mind began to reel.

"I'm not ready for this!" she sobbed. "I don't want to lose him! Not now!
I'm really angry at God!"

And the merciless mind began searching for some way in which his
death was her fault . . . She had screwed up his medications. She had
failed to see the signs. She had failed to challenge the doctors. She had failed
to give him the proper nutrition. She had ignored her gut instincts.

And the doctors became villains. Where was his regular doctor? He
hadn't briefed the on-call doctor sufficiently. They were arrogant. They
didn't listen. They did stupid things. They even admitted that they did
stupid things!

And it felt like her friends had all let her down. And someone who had
promised to be with her that night had just called to cancel!

In general, the message was, "If I hadn't been so lax and the doctors
hadn't been so stupid, Ted would still be alive!"

I said, "You know, Laura, after all we've been through with Ted, I real-
ly have to feel that he was someone who simply could not die one moment
before or one moment after he was supposed to."

And Laura said, "I know that in my mind, but I'm not feeling it right
now."

For nearly two hours one afternoon I sat on the phone and listened
while Laura raged on in one of the most relentless barrages of self-recrimi-
nation, anger, and remorse I have ever attended to.

I said, "Laura, I have never witnessed anyone who was a more devot-
ed and dedicated spouse than you. Your care of Ted has been extraordi-
nary, magnificent, and saint-like. I can't imagine that you feel you were
so inadequate."

She said, somewhat angrily, "I know you and Stephen want me to be
merciful with myself, but I don't feel merciful!"

Finally, in an effort to redirect the energy a bit, I laughed and said,

"Well then, Laura, would it be helpful to you if I just agreed with you that you have screwed up royally? You were a terrible wife, a terrible caretaker, and everybody is outraged at how you neglected Ted!"

She started to laugh.

Her tone softened.

"Well, the truth of the matter is, I know this is all bullshit. But I have to express it . . . it's in my mind. And there are very few people in the world who I would feel comfortable expressing it to."

I had noticed a sense of impatience in my own mind as she had railed on, but I finally realized that she was very consciously dredging up the most difficult and thorny aspects of her grief so that they wouldn't fester inside her and cause problems later. She wanted to grieve fully, now, in the moment . . . to milk yet one more human experience for all it was worth.

I said, "The mercy is the space around these thoughts . . . It's not in pushing these thoughts away or in trying not to have them at all. It's the awareness, which I know you have, that you are a much larger being than these judgmental thoughts are allowing you to feel at the moment."

And then she said, "You know what the most upsetting thing of all is?"

I said, "What?"

"It's that when Ted stopped breathing, a part of me felt relief. I knew it was time. And a little voice inside my head said, 'Good. Thank God it's over.' I haven't expressed that to anyone else. And now I miss him so much."

"And you feel guilty about having that thought?"

"Yes!"

"And Laura, who wouldn't have had that thought after all you've been through? After all . . . thoughts are just thoughts."

And that thought was just one of millions . . . one perfectly natural, yet infinitesimal speck of mind-dust floating momentarily on Laura's ocean of love, compassion, devotion and grief. She adored Ted. She missed him terribly. But there was also some relief. Seeing that relief in her mind, Laura recoiled in horror with the fear that somehow, a thought that arose out of her humanness might dishonor the exraordinary love and devotion she felt for her husband. She had watched him struggle for years. She had worked tirelessly . . . ceaselessly . . .to ensure his well-being. She had consistently sacrificed her own health and comfort to care for Ted. And yet, in one moment of relief, her own mind turned against her. Under the microscope of self-judgment, that infinitesimal speck became a huge cloud of doubt and remorse. At that moment, rather than honor her extraordinary capacity for love, she fell into self-recrimination and guilt.

But those of us who bore witness to her heroic journey know that there will never be any doubt about the profundity and depth of her love for Ted.

*It's amazing how cruel our minds can be to us. We would **never** dream of being as cruel to another human being as we are to ourselves.*

Grief and suffering are with us every moment of our lives. Our births involved suffering, for ourselves and our mothers. Being thrust out of the womb involved suffering. Being a child involves suffering. Being an adolescent involves suffering. Turning twenty involves suffering. Turning thirty involves suffering. Turning forty involves suffering. Fifty . . . sixty . . . seventy . . . eighty . . . Old age involves suffering. Getting what you don't want involves suffering. Even getting what you do want involves suffering because it is in time and form and ultimately will pass away.

All things must pass . . .

Being a parent involves suffering . . . the suffering of seeing your child in pain and being unable to help . . . the suffering of seeing your adolescent do things you know to be self-destructive and being powerless to stop them . . . the suffering of hearing a child say "I hate you" when you have devoted your life to their well-being . . . the suffering of knowing, deep inside, that someday, inevitably, either you will see your child die or your child will see you die. And there is no greater pain on this earth than that of a mother who has seen her child die.

And yet most of these human experiences also contain an element of tremendous joy. A mother endures the excruciating pain of childbirth and labor and at exactly the same moment experiences the incomparable ecstasy of seeing and holding for the first time the precious child that grew inside her. A child enjoys the innocent, nonjudgmental wonder of exploring a new world, of being surrounded (hopefully) by nurturing, caring, and love, and at the same moment experiences frightening, painful childhood diseases, fear of separation from its parents, nightmares, and the pain of growing. An adolescent experiences the euphoric rush of new-found freedom and independence, the thrill of driving a car, and at the same moment the painful insecurity and awkwardness of understanding and integrating the chaotic emotions and sensations of emerging sexuality, trying to find an identity, trying to "measure up," to be acceptable to others. A twenty-year-old may experience the thrill and self-satisfaction of finishing four years of college, only to be thrust into an alien, hostile world of limited job opportunities and millions of people with more qualifications and greater experience. A thirty-year-old may have a spectacular surprise birthday party surrounded by loving friends and family and yet spend most of the time struggling with a gnawing sense that something is wrong . . . that life is speeding by and they still don't know who they are or what they *really* want to do with their life. On and on it goes . . .

A very dear friend of mine recently turned eighty. At her birthday party she gratefully basked in the love and adoration of the friends and relatives who had assembled. She laughed and joked and gave thanks for the fortunate degree of good health she still enjoyed and the number of people who came to honor her and surround her with love. But from time to time her gaze would drift off to some far away place and time. A melancholy would wash over her. A tear or two would drip from her eye. And I could only imagine that she was revisiting all those loved ones who had passed through her life and were no longer with her . . . all of the people she would have wanted to have at her birthday party. How long it had been since she had seen her parents, her husband, her brothers and sister. How many, many deaths she had witnessed. And how long will it be until she'll have to say good-bye to the people who are here now? . . . *And the very next moment she would again be radiant with joy and gratitude.*

You see, grief is always with us. But so is joy. The greatest mistake we make is to assume that if we have one we can't have the other. Both make up the totality of the human experience.

The most joyful people I know are also the ones who can cry the hardest, who are not afraid of their sadness, who open fully to all of the experiences of life. In fact, it might be said that unless one can cry fully, one cannot laugh and love fully. The degree to which we turn off our "negative" feelings will bring an equal diminishing of our "positive" feelings. We can't turn off one part of our being without turning the whole thing off. Then we become emotionally dead. And what could possibly be more destructive to a human life?

We see it most clearly in the medical profession where doctors are *taught* not to become emotionally involved with their patients because—it is assumed—they won't be able to make objective judgments. They'll be overwhelmed and will drown in their natural human concern and compassion. So they are *taught* to turn it off, and once they do, it spills over into the rest of their lives. They are no longer emotionally available for their families and friends. They develop what we've come to refer to as "professional warmth." They *appear* to be caring, but there's an emptiness and insincerity to it all. If ever real feelings start to emerge, they run from the room like there's a bad infection in the air. And like a simmering volcano, they begin to feel this burning, swelling, molten discomfort at the core of their beings that is inevitably bound to erupt in some way at some time.

The irony is that it is not the *acknowledging* of human suffering that causes burnout; it's the *avoidance* of it . . . the pushing away of what is real, of what one is *really* feeling deep inside. It manifests in tremendous fatigue, in anger, in depression, in self-destruction.

But since we have never been given the tools for dealing with it, for the most part we try not to acknowledge it. We've been *taught* not to acknowledge it. How many times were we told as a child, "Don't cry!" And we think we give the greatest compliment to a widow or a widower in grief when we say, "She/he was so *strong* at the funeral. I don't know how she did it. She never shed a tear." We encourage people to "keep a stiff upper lip," mainly because it is so uncomfortable for us to be in the presence of someone who is in overwhelming pain. We don't know how to deal with our own pain, so how can we begin to deal with someone else's?

Stephen Levine often asks, *"Have you ever tried to kiss someone with a stiff upper lip?"*

It's not a particularly nourishing experience.

The most popular responses to grief in our society are methods designed to distract our attention away from the pain. We busy ourselves with other, less emotionally-charged matters. And the greater our pain, the greater the compulsiveness with which we pursue our distractions, be they eating, drinking, collecting, producing, playing, seducing, or bullying.

There is no magic to recognizing that our society's rampant use of emotion-numbing drugs and alcohol springs from our inability and unwillingness to confront and work through the pain in our lives. And isn't it curious that so many of us, who say that we would *never* pollute our systems with drugs and alcohol, claim that we want to live forever, but slowly commit suicide by consuming tobacco and unhealthy foods?

So the "grief" we experience in the wake of a death or loss is really just an amplification of the emotional pain that is always with us. The death or loss temporarily renders our coping mechanisms ineffective and we begin to feel we are drowning in unending sadness, that we may never feel joy again. It's the recognition that no matter how strong, healthy, wealthy, or powerful we are, we can't stop change and death.

In some sense, our fear of life arises both from our recognition of and our desperate fear of inevitable change . . . our knowledge that everything in form ends. As parents, our fears about our children's possible demise can create a kind of paranoid panic that imprisons them. We can force them to live either within the confines of debilitating neuroses that were communicated to them through our fear, or to rebel in ugly ways against our efforts to impose our own limitations on them.

In relationship with others, our fear and insecurity about the long-term prospects for the relationship can lead to a kind of neurotic clinging and efforts toward control that ultimately drive away the very person we sought to keep. Or they can lead us to ignore the inevitable death that will separate us and to putter through life with a pretentious phony sense of blissful ignorance that proves to be our undoing when the inevitable change or demise takes place. We say, *"My God, what a shock. I had no idea there was anything wrong. One day without warning, he was just . . . gone."* I've heard that phrase repeated again and again and again by wives whose husbands left home . . . parents whose children committed suicide . . . and people whose parents have died of a sudden massive heart attack after decades of self-abusing alcohol consumption and cigarette smoking.

Our culture's neurotic denial of death and sadness leads to a fundamental *inattention* to life. We become professional sleepwalkers. And unless we break the pattern, we are condemned to sleepwalk through our entire lives, selectively filtering out all of the abundant information we receive on a daily basis which would have warned us that a cataclysmic change was a real possibility. We push the "negative" information away and smile our way through it all, pretending that when Daddy passed out last night after consuming a fifth of vodka he was just "very sleepy."

> *Habit is a hell to which people cling in an attempt to stop the flow of change.*
> CAROLINE MYSS
> IN *ANATOMY OF THE SPIRIT*

The problem is that we habitually look to external people, places, and things to give us our sense of who we are and to reassure us about the basic "all-rightness" of our being. In psychology this is known as being "other-directed." The desire to "mate" with another usually arises from some sense that we are "incomplete" when we are alone and that our life is essentially a failure if we remain alone.

Most of us would assume that such an impulse is "natural." But the sense that we cannot be fulfilled without having the eyes of another to reflect back to us how wonderful we are on a daily basis is the essential ingredient for disaster in the relationship itself and the foundation of the devastating grief that follows the loss of the relationship.

When we are standing in the middle of the raging fire that is our grief we are in a panic about having lost our connection to that which gave us a sense of order in the Universe, and a sense of meaningfulness in our own existence.

Interestingly, when we say we have "fallen in love" with another human being what we are really saying is that they are "a stimulus that turns us on to the place inside ourselves where we *are* love." Love is an inner experience. It is a state of being. In some traditions it is said to be our *highest* Self.

Most of us spend our entire life searching for other human beings who allow us to feel that love. When we find them, we become addicted to them as if we were drug addicts. For us, they are the "connection." We don't realize that the state of love is inside us . . . we think that another person magically fed something into us that gives us that feeling. So we become dependent and jealous. We desperately fear that they will become a "connection" for someone else and that we will lose them as our "connection." Or we worry incessantly that some danger or illness will befall them. So we seek to control them and possess them. We want to know where they are and what they are doing at all times so that we can prevent them from becoming a "connection" for someone else, or from leaving us through death or volition.

Unfortunately, this fear of change and desire for control ultimately undermine the relationship and our own inherent sense of well-being and security. In our attempt to control other human beings, we are imprisoning them and ourselves.

Our prison is one in which we have communicated to ourselves that we are:

1. **Incomplete**

2. **Disconnected from our own inner resources**

3. **Incapable of happiness without the presence of that other person in our life . . . in the way we want them to be present . . . and with no other beings competing for their attention and affection.**

We have communicated to ourselves that we are dependent and *very* vulnerable.

So when the ultimate separation takes place, through death or volition, we collapse in a heap of despair and hopelessness. We have programmed ourselves for incapacity and disillusionment.

None of this is meant to be communicated as judgment about us as individuals. We have been the recipients of a cultural neurosis about death and a somewhat primitive understanding of love and relationship. In some sense we can be grateful for a loss that gives us the opportunity to explore these issues and the possibility of experiencing ourselves and others in new and deeper ways.

Not that it will be easy. The pain is still there. The despair is still there. The confusion and bewilderment are still there. But this is a starting point. The one thing we have in abundance when we are depressed is *energy*. It's not necessarily the familiar energy that makes us physically vigorous, but the swirling, raging mental patterns that keep us awake at night also represent a potent form of energy.

> *Our work in healing grief is to redirect that energy and to formulate a new perspective on ourselves and on relationship that allows for the possibility of enlightened healing . . . that opens the door for tragedy and suffering to transform us into the larger, more connected, more alive beings that, in truth, we already are.*

LINDA

The first time I saw Linda, I was smitten. It was an experience unlike any I'd ever imagined.

I'm not sure I would call it "love at first sight" but it was profound and overwhelming . . . a deep recognition at the soul level.

I was in graduate school. She was an undergraduate in the same department.

I passed her in the hall late one afternoon near the department's student mailboxes. Suddenly, the earth moved beneath me. There was a palpable sensation I had never felt before. It was like I was being "unplugged" and shaken free from my past.

She was so beautiful. I felt a warm, swirling, cyclic wheel of energy spinning in my chest. We were walking in opposite directions. After a momentary, split-second pause, we continued on our separate ways.

I floated home. I couldn't get her image out of my mind. And the swirling energy in my chest continued throughout the night.

The next day I was sitting on one of those cold, uncomfortable metal folding chairs in a beautiful old wooded gothic lounge at the university listening to a very boring lecture. Suddenly I felt that intensely warm, unfamiliar energy start swirling again in my chest.

I instinctively turned to my left.

*And **there she was** . . . staring straight at me.*

Her eyes were intense, deep brown pools of depth, awareness, and passion.

Our eyes locked. I felt some other energy start spinning at the base of my spine and then quickly rush up into my head. It exploded like one of those Fourth of July rockets that blasts up into the sky and bursts into a shower of multi-colored glittering lights.

I had read about this stuff in books but I had never experienced anything like it before.

Extraordinary, really. After all, this was the kind of thing that was supposed to happen when you met your spiritual teacher or guru. And here I was having it with this incredibly beautiful woman.

*It never occurred to me that she **was** a great spiritual teacher.*

But she was.

*I didn't want to stare at her, but I **had** to meet her.*

When the lecture ended, I turned to where she was sitting.

She was gone.

She had disappeared with the same magical stealth that had brought her into my life and had moved so much spiritual energy inside me.

How could I not have noticed her leaving the room?

I don't know . . . I just didn't.

I was bereft.

Fortunately, we had a mutual friend who introduced us a few days later.

We began dating. She had a boyfriend but he was going to be in Italy for the next nine months. I was just ending a relationship that had been floundering for a couple of years.

She had a wild, uninhibited quality that served as a dramatic counterweight to the stiff, conservative spiritual life I had been leading.

For five years prior to meeting her I had been a celibate yogi. The first four and a half years were hell, but in the final six months I felt my physical cravings start to fall away.

"Aaaahhhh," I thought. "Peace at last . . . I'm finally holy." The austerities had worked. I no longer felt lust.

But then I panicked. I hated it! I was too young to give up being human!

"Good grief! How do I get my lust back?!"

And then I met Linda.

She was so beautiful, and I was so desperate, I think I would have sold my grandmother to be with her.

I ignored the existence of the other boyfriend. I ignored Linda's hesitancy. I often ignored the academic work I had to do if it meant that I could spend time with her.

I pushed, I prodded, I manipulated and cajoled. I showered her with gifts. I took her on beautiful romantic weekend trips. We went out to the most expensive restaurants for candlelit dinners.

She had never experienced any of that before. She became enamored with an entirely new lifestyle.

And I was enamored with her inner freedom, her lack of inhibition, her familiarity with the wild goddess within her, her inexpressible beauty.

*But we were **extremely** different.*

My family and many of my friends disapproved. Linda was generally unconcerned with social propriety, unlike the "refined," more conservative women I had dated earlier in my life.

And then her boyfriend came home from Italy and began showering her with love, unaware of what had been going on between us.

Linda became confused and torn. She said she needed some "space" in order to sort out her confusion. She was being pulled in two directions.

Of course, actually, there were three directions.

Because, in a certain way, she wanted no part of either of us.

I could live with her deciding to stay with me.

I could possibly have come to accept her decision to be alone.

*But I **certainly** could not accept her deciding to go back to him.*

I reluctantly agreed that we should take some time off, so long as she would agree not to be with him on anything other than a Platonic basis while she was deciding.

She promised that would be the case.

But on the very first night of our temporary separation, I drove past her house and his car was there.

Surely she'll send him home, I thought.

But she didn't.

And the earth crumbled beneath me. I was again spinning through the darkest, most inhospitable realms of the Universe.

It was one of the worst nights of my life.

I was in so much emotional pain, I wanted to be dead.

*I tried to sleep, but I couldn't. I would lie down temporarily then realize I was completely incapable of alleviating the painful, searing firestorm of wounded, broken-hearted thoughts. They consumed me and wracked my awareness. It was like a conflagration of psychic pain. I paced around my apartment like a caged animal, reeling in agony at the realization that the deepest, darkest hours of night lay before me and there was **nothing** I could do to get rid of my pain and agitation.*

*At regular sixty-minute intervals, I would dress, go out to my car, and drive over to Linda's house, cruising slowly past to confirm, yet once again, that they weren't just "talking into the wee hours." No, **his** car was still there. **He** was spending the night. The lights were out and had been since about eleven o'clock. My girlfriend's old boyfriend was with her, at* *that moment, right in that house . . . right now, just hours after promising to me that it wouldn't happen.*

I was in complete disbelief.

How could someone—anyone—be so coldly dishonest, so calculatingly cruel, so willing to break their word? On the very first night!

I was shattered.

And all night I paced, I sobbed, and I raged. The hurt and anger danced in and around each other like two rattlesnakes making love.

There was no peace until the first light of dawn when I finally fell asleep, exhausted and spent from living through a real nightmare.

*Oddly enough, at the end of a very painful week, Linda actually chose to leave **him** behind and be with me.*

But now my joy was tempered by a profound distrust.

We embarked on a rocky relationship that would last another year and a half. I wanted to leave it right then but something impelled me onward.

We began to live together but my distrust and paranoia soon began to feel like a prison cage to Linda. I never believed that she was telling me the truth. And I never trusted that she wasn't out seeking other relationships. Whenever she was out of my sight, I was nervous and filled with paranoid fantasies.

Whenever she spoke to another man, or looked at another man, I inwardly became enraged and outwardly became sullen and moody.

It was like living in hell.

The relentless paranoia gave rise to an even more manipulative and controlling side of me which Linda's free-wheeling spirit couldn't tolerate.

So we found ourselves at odds most of the time.

She became more defiantly free-wheeling, while I became more dominant and rigid.

We fought constantly.

Finally, one day she announced she was moving out. In the midst of the sobbing, screaming argument that ensued, she threw a book at me.

It was Wayne Dyer's classic, Your Erroneous Zones.

As she turned to go out the door of our apartment for the last time, she shouted, "Here, read this! You're such a jerk! It might help you!"

A few days later, when the dust had settled, I realized two things:

*I **was** a jerk.*

And I needed help.

I read Wayne's book.

And it not only helped me, it changed my life.

It reminded me that happiness and fulfillment can only come from within. It reminded me that when we attempt to derive happiness from the actions of other people we are doomed to fail. Not only are we doomed to fail, but that very attempt at control may well be the primary cause of dysfunction in relationships.

Your Erroneous Zones was one of those messages that arrived at the right time and in the right place in my life. It became indelibly imprinted on my consciousness.

I have recommended it to dozens of other people since then.

But the dance with Linda wasn't over.

I immersed myself in Wayne's Dyer's teachings. I coupled that with a renewed commitment to meditation practice and spiritual work. I began to back off and allow Linda the space she had always wanted. We began to "date" again.

She responded to the changes in me with warmth and good favor and began to talk about moving back into our apartment again. That was fine with me although I was working diligently not to become attached to the idea and not to return to my old possessive and manipulative ways.

One evening, about five months after Linda had moved out, we went out to dinner. We had been having wonderful times together. She had even stayed over a few nights. We hadn't had an argument in two or three months.

During dinner, Linda casually announced that she had decided to fly to Florida the next day to visit her brother. I said, "Wonderful!" although I was a little perplexed as to why she hadn't told me before this.

I offered to drive her to the airport. She said, "No, my father is going to take me."

I said, "Okay."

Then Linda said, "There's one other thing . . . You can't call me while I'm down there."

"Why not?" I asked.

"Because I need some real time away, just by myself, alone, to think and find my center again. Promise me you won't call me."

I protested a bit but ultimately agreed. One of the most important changes I had made in our relationship was to try to be more accepting of what Linda expressed to be her needs.

Then she said, "But don't worry. I'm feeling really good about us and I'm probably going to move back in with you when I come back." My heart danced.

She went on to tell me how she was planning to redecorate our apartment. I was very happy.

At the end of the evening we kissed and hugged and she went home to her parents' house. I said, "Have a great time with your brother. I'll miss you. Come home safely."

Linda left on a Friday. I honored my commitment not to call her in Florida.

The following Tuesday when I pulled my mail from the mailbox I noticed a letter from Linda. I smiled. My heart warmed. How wonderful that she had already taken the time to write me a love letter! It must be a good sign!

But then I noticed something strange and sinister. There was no return address. And the postmark read "Boulder, Colorado," not "Tallahassee, Florida."

"Oh no!" I thought.

Linda had another old boyfriend in Boulder with whom she had always kept in touch.

I felt a rush of adrenaline surge through me. My legs felt weak. I began to tremble as I tore the envelope open. It was very similar to the way I felt the day Aunt Mabel died.

"Dear John,

"I'm sorry I lied to you. I'm not in Florida and I'm not coming back to New Jersey. Don't blame yourself. It's not your fault. Thank you for all the good times."

Linda

That was it. My mind raced and tumbled and raged. I fell back into that all-too-familiar swirling storm of sadness, disbelief, and anger. "How could she be so coldly cruel? So calculatingly dishonest? What a reprehensible human being! Did she really have to throw in that stuff about moving back in and redecorating the apartment when she knew all along she wasn't coming back?"

Then, just as quickly, I would shift into an extraordinary sadness and regret. I would think the most tender loving thoughts about her. I would feel extraordinary compassion for her. I would realize that if she felt she had to leave me in such a dramatic and deceptive manner, she must have been extraordinarily frightened and intimidated by my earlier anger and manipulative behavior.

I knew inside that I had changed.

And it was clear that outwardly our relationship had changed. But obviously, Linda didn't buy it.

I was heartbroken and filled with shame and regret.

In disbelief, I called Linda's mother. "Where is Linda?" I asked. Her mother stuttered and stammered, finally blurting out, "I begged her not to lie to you, John. She's in Colorado."

"I know," I said. "I just got a letter from her. But is there a phone number or an address where I can get in touch with her?"

Her mother was embarrassed and uncomfortable to be caught in the middle of this. "I'm not supposed to give it to you, John." And then, not knowing what else to do, she said, "But why don't you come to dinner tomorrow night?"

Her parents and I had a very nice evening together. Her mother even prepared her famous roast duck, which I loved. And, in the end, her mother gave me the address in Boulder. But she said, "Please don't go there or call. Linda would never forgive me. But I guess it's okay to write."

I went home and wrote all night. A twenty-page handwritten letter full of love and passion and regret. It wasn't finished until after dawn. I mailed it that morning as the post office was opening.

But there was no response.

A week later I wrote another twenty pager.

Still no response.

Finally I realized that, knowing Linda as I did, the letters were probably just getting tossed into the garbage can unopened.

It was one of the most frustrating, gut-wrenching experiences I have ever had.

I had so much to say, and no way to say it.

It was as if she had fallen off the face of the earth.

And I was in a peculiar predicament. I had just lost a relationship that had caused us both extraordinary misery. But I was still suffering.

And at some level, Linda's abrupt and calculating cruelty also had the effect on me of a great Zen teaching.

After all, like the great unsolvable koans intended to burn out the judging, rational mind of the student, Linda's behavior defied all reason and understanding. She had taken my world and turned it upside down and inside out. She had acted in an incomprehensible fashion, like any great Zen master would.

And although, at the human level, we had both exhibited behavior that was inexcusable, at the spiritual level her "rape" of my consciousness and sensibilities was just what I needed at that moment.

I saw the irony of being in the midst of one of the most painful experiences of my life . . . and feeling tremendous relief.

So I surrendered.

There was always the option of flying to Boulder and trying to find her. But that seemed overly dramatic and futile. The message was clear: It was over.

From the beginning, our relationship had been fraught with difficulty, conflict, and distress. At some level I don't think either one of us really wanted the relationship, but something inside us both impelled us to keep it going. Some desire or set of desires or emotional needs caused us both to override our intuition and our instincts and keep it going.

And that was the core problem. In our deepest souls, neither Linda nor I wanted to be with each another in a romantic relationship. So every moment we spent together was a moment in which we were both out of sync with our inner beings.

There is simply no way to be sane, rational, loving, or compassionate if you are out of sync with your inner being.

I realized a cruel irony—throughout my life, whenever I had been in a relationship, I didn't want to be. And whenever I wasn't in a relationship, I wanted to be.

I had been leading a totally schizophrenic existence.

Since I was no longer in a relationship, I decided that I should explore the part of me that didn't want to be.

What was it in me that wanted to be alone much of the time, that sometimes resented other people in my "space?" What was it in me that often wanted just to be alone to meditate? What was it in me that previously had just wanted a solitary, celibate existence?

Those questions gave rise to a very interesting period of my life.

I expanded my meditation practice and once again began practicing yoga. I read holy books and chanted. My life became an extended prayer. I bought a camper van and traveled around the country alone, visiting spiritual communities and spending time in nature. I actually began "camping out" for the first time in my life.

I spent many nights in the camper, alone, in campgrounds, on mountains, and in forests all over the country with nothing but the sounds of the crickets, the birds, the forest animals, the rustling of the leaves in the trees, the soft rush of wind, and my own breath.

I began to spontaneously meet people. And when I spent time with women, I no longer had to immediately judge and evaluate their worthiness to be my partner.

I didn't want a partner. I no longer had to evaluate how physically attractive I found them. I could just see them as unique and fascinating individuals whose life stories and experiences were always a joy to hear. It completely changed the character of my interactions with women.

It was during that period that I began spending a lot of time with Ram Dass. And he served as a kind of alternative role model. He had found success and happiness in a similar life style and, by example, validated what I was doing and feeling.

It was one of the happiest periods of my life. I moved through each day on instinct, following my intuition. I learned how to "feel" my way through life rather than "thinking" my way through.

And I recognized that the reason the other people in my life had so often felt like they were in the way was because the entanglements of social, familial, and romantic relationships consumed so much of my consciousness. There was little room left for inner exploration.

And now, in the solitude I had embraced, the "inner being" could emerge.

Amazingly enough, I never felt alone. Each morning when I awoke to greet the sunrise, I felt full, more full than I had ever felt before.

And I recognized that the motivation to be alone emerged from the yearning of my Soul . . . to be known . . . to be recognized . . . to be acknowledged.

And I yearned to let my soul, my inner being, my essential core come into the light of awareness, to infuse each moment of my life with peace, fulfillment, and meaning.

Of all the miracles in my life, that "awakening" may have been the greatest.

Ten months after Linda's departure, Christmas was approaching. I sent her a card. I suggested that if she was coming home to New Jersey for the holidays I would love to get together with her. I prepared myself for the possibility that the card might end up in the garbage can with the rest of my letters . . . and there would be no response.

But to my surprise, one evening just a few days before Christmas, the phone rang and there she was!

"Hello, John!" she said in her customary impish voice. "I'm in New Jersey and if you want to get together it might be nice."

The next day we met at her parents' house and went for a walk in the woods. In a clearing we stopped and sat on a huge boulder to rest for a while.

So far we had busied ourselves with small talk and gossip, skillfully skirting around all of the difficult, edgy issues between us.

Finally, I said, "Why don't we talk a little bit about what happened?"

Linda seemed hesitant. "What for?" she asked. "What possible good could it do?"

I said, "Maybe, if we both understood what happened a little better, we could avoid making the same kind of mistakes in the future."

She crinkled up her nose as if the memories resembled a foul odor. "Maybe . . ." I could see she was unconvinced.

So I took the lead. I confessed that I had never acted more horribly in a relationship. That I was consumed with paranoia, mistrust, and discontent throughout the relationship. And further, I confessed that if I hadn't been celibate for five years prior to meeting her and if she hadn't been so beautiful, I would never have gotten involved with her in anything more than a friendship.

She seemed to find the candor refreshing, so she got into the same spirit. She confessed that her behavior had been awful. And she said, essentially, that if I hadn't been able to provide all the gifts, vacations, and financial freedom, she would have never gotten involved in anything other than a friendship with me.

It all became clear. I started laughing out loud.

"What's so funny?" she asked.

I said, "Well, there it is, Linda: lust and greed. Our entire relationship was built on lust and greed! No wonder it was such a mess!"

We laughed and hugged. She said, "So why don't we just be friends? We're really good at that."

And since that day we have had an extraordinary connection.

And I have never forgotten that relationship based on anything other than mutual love, and respect, and the ability to engender a shared purpose in life . . . is doomed to failure.

Even when those qualities *are* present, relationship is, as Stephen and Ondrea have pointed out, "the most difficult yoga there is."

> *The most profound question is,*
> *"How do we find peace amidst the chaos?"*

Chapter Twelve

FINDING PEACE:
SOME CLUES ALONG THE WAY

We have begun a journey. A journey into our minds. A journey of discovery and exploration of who and what we are. Taking the first step is difficult . . . The spiritual quest we are embarking on is a rare and precious undertaking, so be gentle, yet persevering through any difficulties . . . We're ascending the mountain of spiritual insight. We have already discovered the secret of its invisibility: The fact that the truth, the law . . . is within us, not outside of ourselves . . .

JOSEPH GOLDSTEIN
IN *THE EXPERIENCE OF INSIGHT*

A T SOME POINT IN OUR LIVES, EACH OF US HAS EXPERIENCED MOMENTS of calm fulfillment, moments when everything seemed "okay," when our instinctive trust in the Universe came to the surface and we let down our guard and our defenses. We felt warmth, we felt peace, we felt contentment. We breathed in deeply, our abdomens unusually relaxed, our shoulders uncharacteristically low. We breathed out a long liberating exhale. "Aaaahhhhhhhhh." The subtle fear was gone. The wariness had melted. The confusion and doubt had receded into irrelevance. We felt connected. We felt complete. We felt whole.

Some would say it felt like being in our mother's arms . . . or back in the womb. Some would say it felt like a sense of "oneness" with nature or with the Universe. Some would say they forgot all their cares and just "let go." Some would say it's the experience we were born for . . . the "peace that passeth all understanding."

For a mother, it may have come through the experience of childbirth, of bringing another human being into the world. For others it may have come through romance. It may have come through a winning athletic effort or an outstanding artistic performance. Perhaps it came through scuba diving . . . through skydiving . . . through a scientific breakthrough . . . through sex . . . through mountain climbing . . . or just sitting by a stream . . . or on the beach. It may have come at the moment we fell in love . . . or at the moment we lay in the grass staring up at the stars in the nighttime sky. It may have come in meditation or in prayer. . . that evening in Paris . . . the gondola ride in Venice . . . the picnic in Central Park . . . being caressed and kissed by a school of fish while snorkeling. . . the motorcycle ride down Pacific Coast Highway . . . the moment he said, "I love you."

At these moments, we transcend our limitations. And the state of expansiveness we move into *is* love. Since we have no fear, we have no anger, because the two are intricately intertwined. When we're "in love" even people we *don't* like are suddenly okay. We may feel compassion for their predicament. There's no attraction to negativity because it separates and divides and we are *so* content in our experience of merging.

But that very recognition, when the mind begins to focus on it, is terrifying. We've let down our defenses! "My God, I've allowed myself to be vulnerable! I am unprotected! I am out of my mind!"

"Come back to earth!" we tell ourselves. "Get hold of yourself!" "Come to your senses!"

And suddenly we are again separate and frightened. We return to the comfortable familiarity of our fears. We sacrifice bliss and joy and aliveness to feel "safe." For a moment our minds quieted and our hearts opened and we expanded into larger, less defined beings, with a spirit of playfulness and freedom, but as soon as our minds "kicked in" they told us we were in unsafe territory.

We remember the experience and we desperately want to recapture it. The problem is that we are using our minds to create the experience again . . . and our minds want to come along this time. We want the bliss, but we also want the "safety" of our judging minds.

So we become addicted to whatever the method was that got us into that state of expanded awareness in the first place. We want to do it all the time. And if it was a person who got us there, we want to be with them all the time and to protect them and ensure that they won't fall into danger . . . or the arms of another.

Our grief is the agony that is generated by this effort to control. It's the conceptualizing of a "perfect" Universe, one in which everything and everyone is just as we want them to be . . . and then the resistance to the way they really are.

If we think back on our moments of bliss and contentment, we would very likely remember that they came unexpectedly, not as a result of something we had designed for ourselves, but as a result of a surprising development, an unforeseen turn of events and emotions. We may have practiced our golf swing for years, but the day we first broke 80 on the golf course our feelings of intense satisfaction are experienced not so much as the "end result" of all our preparation, but rather as *a magical unlocking of the doorway to fulfillment inside us that had previously been sealed shut.*

Similarly, when we "fall in love" the feeling often washes over us at an unexpected moment. It is a "high" unlike any we've ever felt. And though the physical and mental images of our beloved are connected to the unfolding of the experience, that experience is still *inside* of us.

The foundations of our grief are built in our mind's misperception that the experience of love was fed into us from outside—that we can *only* have it if the person who triggered it is present in our life in the way we want them to be or the circumstances of our life are exactly as we have designed them in our minds.

We don't acknowledge how vulnerable we are . . . we want things the way we want them. We don't recognize the improbability of our lives—and the people in them—working out the way we want them to. It's almost as if we constantly climb up a tree on the edge of a cliff, make our way out to a thin, fragile branch that overhangs the canyon, jump up and down on that skinny, fragile branch, and then shout out, *"I'm going to be really upset if this branch breaks and I fall into the chasm."*

In so many ways, we construct the conditions of our own suffering and then, when the suffering comes, we feel victimized by some outside force, or power, or individual.

Sometimes the grief in a relationship comes because a state of love, acceptance, and fulfillment was *never* achieved. Many of us have had extremely difficult relationships with our parents. If that is the case, our lives come to revolve, often subconsciously, around the process of attempting to resolve and complete whatever conflicts and incompleteness exist in those relationships.

It is possible and even common for an individual to spend an entire lifetime in a profound state of discontent, driven by an emptiness that dates back to some slight, some series of slights, or some offense that one or the other parent committed during the child's early years. A woman may spend her entire adult life habitually, mechanically sleeping with man after man after man all because her "inner child" longs for a love, affection, and acceptance she never got from her father.

And a man may spend decades amassing a fortune but never achieving happiness because he is driven to disprove a father who told him he would "never amount to anything." At some level, no matter how much money he has, he still fears that he "doesn't amount to anything."

It is equally plausible that the same man might spend every day of his adult life sitting in barrooms and consuming a quart of Jack Daniels all because he believed his father.

Our grief may also arise out of the awareness, real or imagined, that we have lost the *possibility* of having a good relationship because of age, illness, or being physically challenged.

If our sense of meaning in life has arisen from our ability to produce and achieve, the process of retirement may bring on a profound experience of grief as we wrestle with a loss of identity and direction. It's as if we don't know who we are or what life means if we aren't in constant motion.

For years I have carried around a full page ad I cut out of a magazine. It's an ad for Rolls-Royce Motor Cars. It features a photograph of two cars stopped at a traffic light in Beverly Hills. One is a $90,000 BMW and the other is a $250,000 Rolls Royce. The very well-dressed man behind the wheel of the BMW is looking longingly at the Rolls Royce. The caption reads, "Rolls Royce . . . Quite Simply the Best Motor Car in the World." But I have always felt the caption should be, "It's Never Enough."

Over the course of my life I have had the opportunity to know and spend a lot of time with some very wealthy people. And, in most circumstances, the old clichés hold true. Money does not buy happiness. I know some extremely wealthy people who are extremely confused and miserable. And it *is* never enough. Most people in the world are convinced that if they had more money, their worries would disappear. But people who have money suffer from an extraordinary fear of losing it . . . or worrying that it's not enough, that they need more and more and more to keep pace with inflation and to avoid suffering embarrassment as their friends, neighbors, and associates ascend higher and higher.

We look with awe upon those people in our society who we define as "driven." We admire them and compare ourselves to them, often wishing that we could cultivate the same level of "ambition" and dedicate ourselves to the same degree of accomplishment.

While it is possible to be single-mindedly devoted to a cause for humanitarian or philanthropic reasons or for the fulfillment of some personal dream or vision, more often people who are "driven" are motivated by some deep inner turmoil and sense of emptiness. Their manic drive to achieve and accomplish really grows out of a need to relieve their own inner discontent—their grief—in much the same manner as someone of a different temperament might be inclined to drink their troubles away.

Substance abuse and addiction, sexual addiction, power addiction, money addiction—all of these are expressions of unresolved grief, of a profound sense of loss and incompleteness.

I don't mean to suggest that there is no value in hard work. Nor do I mean to suggest that we shouldn't, at times, dedicate ourselves with a one-pointed focus toward the accomplishment of some heartfelt dream or the realization of some extremely meaningful personal goal.

Hard work, discipline, and the ability to be focused are essential, invaluable tools for accomplishing one's life purpose, for leading a life that feels "full" and "meaningful" rather than "empty." *The irony is that only through discipline can we achieve freedom.*

One of the greatest griefs we can experience is the sense that we did less than we were capable of . . . in our relationships, in our world, and in our efforts to accomplish whatever our hearts encouraged us to accomplish.

Simply stated, when we die or a loved one dies, as we reflect on our life, or our relationship, we are usually much less concerned about what we *did* than about what we *didn't* do.

On the other hand . . . as has been stated so often in recent years, when we are on our deathbed we are usually not wishing we had spent more time at the office.

The key is to find a balance, to find fulfillment in *everything* we do rather than to "sleepwalk" through life neglecting things and people who are important to us, mindlessly striving for an elusive sense of "success" and "achievement."

Responsible, focused management of finances can eliminate much of the debilitating stress that surrounds financial hardship. It is not evil to make money, and it is wise to save it.

But the "drive" we see in many people often arises out of less healthy, less conscious motives.

In general, everything our culture has told us and taught us about grief has exacerbated the problem rather than relieving it. In order to "heal" through this experience, we must unlearn much of what we learned about dealing with grief. Rather than pushing it away, rather than pretending it's not present, rather than keeping a stiff upper lip, we need to have the courage to cry, to sob, to open our hearts and allow ourselves to experience the pain, the rage, the frustration, the anger, the profound sadness. We need to know that we will not drown in it all. We may go under for a while, but we won't drown if we stay connected to our hearts.

Our hearts are our lifeline. If we react in fear and close them, we lose the healing potential and solace they offer. Our hearts have no boundaries—they are infinite. The only boundaries they have are the ones our minds impose on them.

The healing of grief begins when we allow our hearts to be open and vulnerable, when we allow ourselves into them, and allow our wounds and sorrows to be healed by them. While our cultural conditioning has been to close our hearts at times of sadness or fear, the true healing takes place when we open them to absorb our darkness, and swallow it into the infinite light they contain.

The miracle is that our very own hearts offer us the opportunity for growth, for completeness, for forgiveness, for nurturing, and for the realization of infinite opportunities.

So *Real* fulfillment is found inside ourselves.

It *really* isn't dependent on the presence of, or actions of, anyone else.

It *really* isn't dependent on the acquisition of material possessions and wealth.

Each loss,
each place of emptiness,
each unresolved grief,
every resentment,
and every failure
can be healed in
the infinite mercy of our own hearts.

Chapter Thirteen

BUT HOW DO I DO THAT?

"OH SURE," YOU SAY. *"WHAT TRIVIAL NONSENSE. WHAT A THIN, SYRUPY, pie-in-the-sky notion. Heal ourselves with our own hearts! Sure! I'm far too miserable. I can't even feel my heart . . . and when I do, it's just a cold, aching, empty hole. My life is over . . . it's meaningless. I'll never be the same. I'm not even sure I know what love is!"*

Many of us have a painfully diminished sense of self-esteem. We have spent a lifetime trying to use externals to override our inner sense of unworthiness. We measure our value in terms of how much we can accomplish, who will spend time with us, and how much time they will spend.

We move from one activity to another and one relationship to another like a hiker crossing a stream—cautiously stepping on one stone at a time, careful not to move off the one we're on until we've spotted another and safely navigated the transition. We don't want to fall in the water . . . we don't want to step into the cold, clammy, murky unknown just beneath the surface of consciousness.

When we face a cataclysmic loss we may try to remain on the

stones above the surface but the raging currents ultimately wash over us and drag us under. We find ourselves, at last, exactly where we have tried for so long not to be. Ironically, it is within the raging torrents of emotion that we have kept submerged all these years that we can finally begin the work of coming fully into our lives.

In nursing schools, departments of social work, departments of psychology, hospitals, cemeteries, and funeral homes, some of the most often asked questions from students and new members of the staff are, "How do I deal with families who become emotional, who are overcome with grief? What do I say? How do I act? How do I keep from breaking down myself?"

When we have to go to a funeral, visit a sick friend in the hospital, or see someone who had a recent loss, we ask ourselves the same questions.

The answer to how we deal with grief in others is always the same. We must first deal with our own. Unless we have consciously dealt with the anger, confusion, and despair brought on by loss in our own lives and have made space for them in our hearts, we will have no room for the pain others feel and no clue about how to help them. The principle is, unless we know how to swim, we can't save someone who's drowning.

The first step is to begin to allow for the possibility that death and loss are not mistakes . . . to allow for the possibility that, even in the midst of apparent chaos, there is order and natural law at work in the Universe. Even the sudden tragic death of a loved one or the death of a child may, if we can stay open to the experience, provide the opportunity to break through all kinds of psychological and spiritual barriers and pave the way for a new, deeper experience of life—a dramatic re-ordering of priorities. Stephen Levine refers to this process as *"keeping your heart open in hell."*

Not that we would wish these experiences on anyone. But we are all aware that from time to time human beings are confronted with hellish circumstances in their lives. That we would prefer for circumstances to be other than they are is natural. However, the ability to deal with the circumstances of life "as they are," to deal with "what is" rather than to yearn for what we wish "had been," is the key to unlocking the grip that the emotional pain has on us.

We react to death and loss as "unfortunate," "incomprehensible," and "wrong." But death just is. It is a fact of life. All forms change, decay, and die. *All* forms.

> *The thought that our life should be other than it is at **this** moment, that the circumstances of our life, our family, our business, our world are unacceptable, is the groundwork of our grief. Any thought that takes us out of **this** moment, whatever feelings and experiences **this** moment may hold, is the groundwork of our grief. The life and death issues in this Universe ultimately are beyond our control. We can be prudent, responsible, careful, and protective of ourselves and our loved ones, but ultimately it is all beyond our control.*

Ironically, we sometimes unconsciously worship the process of change that takes place in the natural Universe. For years I have made it a tradition to spend a long weekend in Vermont every October. When I am there, I marvel at the tens of thousands of people who come to witness the beauty of the decaying leaves . . . the transition from the verdant green summer to the cold, barren winter. The chill in the air and the discoloring, dying leaves that fall in huge piles on the ground, are what the tourists come to see and experience. But few of them would ever stop to acknowledge that they are making a pilgrimage to witness and honor death and decay.

In India, the One God, Brahman, is also worshipped as a trinity that includes three important aspects: Brahma (the Creator), Vishnu (the Preserver), and Shiva (the Destroyer). One of the shortcomings of western culture has been the focus on creation and preservation without a concomitant awareness of the role of destruction in the natural order of the Universe.

Twenty-five years ago when I first started spending time with people who were terminally ill, I began to hear something that astounded me. It turned my perception of the Universe inside out. A significant percentage (not a majority, but a significant minority) of the cancer patients I spent time with said something like, *"I've never felt as alive as I do since I found out I have cancer."*

Wow! *What did that mean? Where were they coming from?*

What I started to realize was that when we consciously *know* we are mortal, when we consciously know that we have a finite time line, the priorities in our lives and the way we live them start to change dramatically. We *really* start to pay attention . . . to our relationships, to our surroundings, to each moment of this precious existence. We hear sounds we've never heard before, we see sights we've never seen before, we taste tastes we've never tasted before. We notice the exquisite complexity of the human body. We rejoice in the ability to walk. We feel the ecstasy of being able to breathe. We revel in the caress of the wind, the sound of the rain, the warmth of the sun. Most of all, we recognize that we have no time to waste. We realize that our relationships must be loving, healthy, conscious, and alive *NOW!*

Most of us postpone being fully alive. We think that happiness and fulfillment are something we will reach later, when we graduate, when we get a good job, when we have enough money in the bank, when we meet the perfect mate, when we close the big deal, when we retire.

But how many people die each year who didn't make it to retirement? How many people do we know who kept themselves so busy, so obsessed with activity, accomplishment, and stimulation, that the only opportunity they gave themselves to slow down and rethink their goals came when they were lying in a hospital bed following their heart attack or bypass surgery? And how many people have I spoken to who, when dying in their sixties, seventies, and eighties, said, "I don't know what my life was all about. I always thought it was something that was going to happen *later."*

Our world and our news media give us the opportunity to stay tuned to the uncertain and temporary quality of human life. Every day could be our last, or the last for someone we love. We need to live our lives as if we know that. We've been taught that to think that way would paralyze us, would make us depressed and incapable of acting, but just the opposite is the case. Recognizing our mortality is what urges us and prompts us to be *fully alive* every day. Hiding from that truth is what numbs us and paralyzes us. It turns us into robots who don't see or accept the totality of the Universe we live in.

Living in this reality is absolutely life-changing. As we said at the beginning of Chapter Eleven, we become aware that much of grief is the remorse over lost opportunities, the sense of incompleteness. It is the recognition that someone we care for has died and we feel that we never knew them fully, that we never accepted them completely into our hearts, that our connection was not as fulfilling as we, or they, wanted it to be. The work of healing our grief is the work of learning how to complete those aspects of the relationship after the other person is no longer physically available.

Why not do it now with those in our life who are still alive?

EXERCISE

There is a simple ritual you can perform whenever you part from your loved ones: Take a moment to recognize that you may never see each other again. Therefore your kiss or your hug or your glance must communicate all the devotion and love you feel for each other—all the gratitude you feel for having had the opportunity to be together all these years.

Eventually this can become so much a part of your relationship that you no longer need to say it. It's all communicated non-verbally, but it keeps your relationships very, very much alive.

Your relationships would also benefit greatly from a commitment never to part in anger. If the other person in the relationship is willing, make a commitment to one another that if there is a problem, a moment of anger, you will stay and work it through until you can part in love. We have seen over the years that if the final interaction with a loved one was one of anger, the grieving process can become much more complicated.

When I make these suggestions in lectures, people often respond by saying, "Oh, that must be so depressing! How can you be happy when you're constantly thinking of death?" But that question comes from our cultural conditioning.

*In fact, nothing inspires us to want to find true happiness more effectively than thinking about our own mortality, and nothing else can communicate the urgency with which we need to pursue deeper levels of love and the sense of **being fully alive**.*

Chapter Fourteen

"Working with the Death of a Parent"

Not until the parent dies is the child fully born.

This statement may sound cold, cruel, heartless, confusing. But let me explain:

At some level, we live much of our adult lives in a subordinate relationship to our parents. Our bodies, and personalities, were molded by them. We are, in a very real sense, their creation, physically, mentally, and emotionally.

Our parents implanted their genes in us. They shaped the environment we were born into. They taught us how to communicate. They helped us learn to move.

They surrounded us with a value system. They showed us how to interact with the world and each other. They showed us what was right and what was left. They showed us what was "right" and what was "wrong."

At various times, we fulfilled our role as children by turning against what we had been taught. We asserted our individuality. We defined ourselves by rejecting our parents' beliefs, values, and behavior.

At other times, we've made it our business to mirror them . . . to become a replica of what they were . . . to espouse what they stood for.

As we get older, we may realize that we have never fully emerged from their shadow. We may begin to have moments when we hear our parents speaking through us. We may see them acting through us. We may look in the mirror and see our bodies turning into theirs.

When we are young, we "parrot" our parents. Later in life we feel them in our souls. We act and speak as they would—in spite of ourselves.

There are moments when we feel pride about that. And there are moments when we feel nightmarishly deranged and possessed.

Some of us honor our parents for making us what we are. Some of us curse them.

Some of us do both.

Some of us honor one and curse the other.

Many of us love our parents dearly. Many of us long for a love that was never there.

So the death of a parent is a very complicated issue.

In a very real sense, parts of us are dying too.

And our love for that parent will cry out in fear and sadness as our minds try in vain to cling to what used to be.

And the ways in which the relationship feels unfulfilled will give rise to a subtle panic as we confront the possibility that our parent will die without ever helping us resolve that which remains unresolved.

And we begin to feel an eerie, uncomfortable loss of safety as we realize that if our parents are vulnerable, so are we.

At times, we question the wisdom and benevolence of a Universe that would allow suffering . . . that would take away our protector, our life-long companion, our friend, in such a cruel manner.

And our culture, obsessed as it is with eternal youth, has given us little preparation for the inevitable physical parting that must take place.

So we look upon the myriad of methods our Universe employs to take the life out of a human form as mistakes, as aberrations. Parents aren't supposed to die. Parents aren't supposed to die like that.

The death of a parent is a very complicated issue.

For many of us, the first time we truly encounter death and grief is when one of our parents dies. We often feel totally unprepared. We can't comprehend it. No matter how old, or educated, or rational we are, when a parent dies we are confronted with a myriad of difficult and confusing thoughts and emotions.

We often say that there is no pain greater than the pain of a parent losing a child. And that is absolutely true. Part of that pain stems from the emotional belief that it is a violation of the natural order of things. Children aren't supposed to die before parents. But they sometimes do . . .

Ironically, as children, we also often feel a resentment or confusion about seeing our parents die. After all, no matter how much of our lives we may have already lived, our parents are the ones who have always been there. Our first relationships were formed with our parents. They are the ones who conceived us, who gave us birth, who cared for us and nurtured us, who raised us and guided us and protected us.

Most of us will feel a strange, somewhat surprising sadness and vulnerability when a parent dies. Even in our twenties or thirties, our forties, fifties, or sixties, when a parent dies there is still, somewhere inside . . . no matter how faint . . . the voice of the inner child begging, *"Mommy, please don't die . . . Daddy, please don't die!"*

Most of us don't know where that voice comes from, and many of us can barely recognize it. But as John Bradshaw and others tell us, our inner child is always with us and it can wreak havoc if it is left unattended and unacknowledged.

The death of a parent, like all deaths we face, can come in any number of ways. It can come suddenly, the result of an accident, a heart attack, or a stroke. It can come with a little warning, as in the case of various short-term illnesses, or the ultimate result of an accident. Or it can come, as it will for most, as the result of a long-term illness.

Our parents will die. And we will die. And our parents' deaths can be yet one more in a lifetime of teachings and guidance they have given us.

But the old statement "One dies as one lives" applies to our parents as much as to everyone else. If our parents were irascible and difficult during their lives, they will probably become even more so as they approach their deaths. If they were wise and equanimous during their life, they will likely become more so as they approach their death. They may be an inspiring example of how to work with the inevitable aging and decay of their body, or they may be, rather, a startling example of what we don't want to become.

Either way, our parents will continue to be examples for us—examples we want to follow, or examples we don't want to follow—but examples nonetheless . . . pioneers blazing the trails ahead of us, leading the way and pointing out, either through insight or example, the pitfalls and pratfalls that await us further down the paths of our lives.

When my father was dying of lung cancer a number of years ago, I spent a lot of time talking with Stephen Levine about what I was feeling. At one point, Stephen turned to me and said, "Maybe your father isn't going to die at all . . . maybe *you* are. Maybe all of your work with your father is preparation for your own death."

It was an interesting juxtaposition. How many times had I heard stories from people in families where just such a figure-ground reversal had happened. Where one member of the family was working with a life-threatening or terminal diagnosis and another member of the family had suddenly, unexpectedly, predeceased the sick one.

You see, we have no guarantees in this life.

There is no power that can guarantee that you or I are going to live one more minute.

DON JUAN IN *JOURNEY TO IXTLAN*
BY CARLOS CASTENEDA

When a parent ages and approaches death, one of the most diffi-cult issues for a child to deal with, no matter what the relative ages of the parent and child are, is the almost inevitable return to a child-like state as one approaches death. To see a parent lose the ability to walk, to hear, to see, to remember . . . to lose weight and energy . . . to need to be fed and bathed and clothed . . . to lose control of their bladder and bowels . . . to need to be cared for as one would care for an infant . . . all of this can be extremely upsetting and unsettling for a child.

But I can tell you from my own experience that if you can sur-render all your doubt and judgment about the wisdom or lack there-of in the Universe, if you can just allow for the possibility that what's happening is not a mistake, but is rather a natural process that mir-rors the pattern of birth, growth, preservation, decay, and destruc-tion which permeates the entire physical Universe . . . if you can accept that you are part of a cycle in which your parents gave birth to you, raised you, nurtured you, fed you, bathed you, carried you around before you could walk, and changed your diapers . . . and that as life progresses, you may, later in life—if you are fortunate— have the opportunity to do the same for them, then your interaction with your parents may provide you with one of the most richly rewarding opportunities a human life can offer.

There is an old saying that goes, "Once an adult, twice a child." It is a profoundly simple summary of the course of a human life.

When a parent is dying we have an opportunity to meet each other in a new way, a way we may have never dreamed possible. We have an opportunity to finish business, to complete our relationship, to explore the unexplored areas, and to bring love and acceptance into areas where they may have been painfully absent.

If the parent is willing and able to share in the exploration and journey, the process of preparing to leave their body can bring parent and child into a relationship that transcends all previous boundaries, that forges a connection that is truly inspirational. When the previous roles and postures fall away, parent and child can experience the ways in which they are one, behind their bodies and personalities, in the shared heart of love each had always longed for.

Even if the parent is unable, due to physical or emotional factors or deteriorated mental capacities, to fully participate in the dialogue and the melting of boundaries, the child can, on her or his own, do extraordinary work toward coming into the fullness and connectedness they had always hoped for.

The irony is that the death of a parent can be the catalyst for developing the relationship with that parent and, ultimately, with oneself that had been elusive earlier in life. The death of a parent can, if dealt with in openness and honesty, bring forth an enhanced sense of strength, clarity of purpose, and a greatly enhanced capacity to live life and to love fully, rather than leaving an empty void in one's heart.

Chapter Fifteen

My Father's Deaths

DURING THE COURSE OF MY FATHER'S LIFE HE AND I WENT THROUGH *many, many different levels of relationship, some joyous, some horrifying. His death provided the opportunity to explore many more levels we hadn't previously touched.*

Before I was born, he had been a terrible alcoholic. His behavior had corroded his marriage to my mother and badly impacted his relationship with my older sisters.

But he had prayed for years to have a son and shortly after I was born he decided to clean up his life as an expression of gratitude that his prayers had been answered. He checked into an alcohol rehab program at Fair Oaks Hospital in Summit, New Jersey, and spent the first eleven years of my life absolutely sober.

As a child, I had no conscious memories of his drinking and instead knew him only as my favorite person—my hero, my best buddy, my "pal." I wanted to be just like him—to look like him, to talk like him, to dress like him, to spend all my time with him, to please him. He was everything I wanted to be.

Then when I was eleven, he took a job as vice president and national sales manager for a large corporation. Though the job gave him a big income and a lot of prestige, his new lifestyle took a toll on the family. In the first year he spent 320 days on the road. We hardly ever saw him. While he was off traveling, he began to drink again. After a while, his business trips evolved into extended binges and sometimes we wouldn't know where he was for weeks at a time.

Not long thereafter, he began drinking at home, in front of us, and when he did, his behavior bordered on demonic. When he was sober, he was one of the most congenial, friendly, kind, and easygoing people on earth. When he was drunk, he was a horrifyingly angry being who was filled with seething paranoia and resentment. He bellowed uncontrollably and unceasingly. He hated everyone, especially my mother, my sisters, and me. And he was convinced that we hated him.

The next day, when he was sober, he would be remorseful, guilty, and apologetic . . . and then he would drink again.

At times, after hours of badgering and berating all of us, he would fall into a chair and cry in great heaving sobs of agony while endless rivers of tears ran down his cheeks and fell from his chin. It was heart wrenching and unbelievably confusing to me. I became frozen in an emotional purgatory.

I remember feeling that my father was inhabited by a demon. A dark, sinister, angry, hateful soul from the nether world would burst forth as soon as the alcohol loosened the bars of his cage.

As I got older, I realized that my father spent his life wrestling with some great sadness and disappointment from his past . . . perhaps from his childhood. To this day my sisters and I have no idea what it was. He was filled with anger and self-hatred when he was drunk. And underneath the anger and self-hatred was some of the most extraordinary pain I have ever witnessed a human being experiencing.

When his friends saw that side of him they never forgot it. It was such a dramatic contrast to the exceptionally wonderful, cheerful, positive human being they knew when he was sober.

My mother taught me about dying. But no one in my life taught me more about grief than my father.

When his drinking behavior started I spent most nights crying hysterically while I watched him and my mother engage in vicious arguments that ripped our loving, caring, happy family to shreds. I began to feel like I was the most mature and wise person in the house. That's a problem when you're the youngest.

So I resolved that in order to survive, I would have to stop feeling. It was a conscious choice. Soon there were no more tears. I taught myself to relate to my father with a cold, cynical detachment.

From the time I was 14 until I was 18, I avoided sitting in the same room with him. I couldn't stand the sight of him, the sound of his voice, or the ever-present smell of liquor on his breath.

I would pray that he would just go away and stay away. When he was hungover and violently ill I would secretly rejoice and take pleasure in his suffering. I suppose my feelings toward him eventually bordered on hatred.

Years later, when I was in my early thirties, I finally realized that the anger I felt was, in truth, a reaction to the profound sadness and helplessness that tore my heart apart. To watch the person I most loved and admired turn into a tortured, tormented lunatic, to feel his normally warm and awesome heart close so abruptly, so completely, sometimes on a daily basis, to see him raving one minute and sobbing the next, and to be powerless to do anything about it was the most devastating experience of my life.

It was my awakening to grief. My grief . . . and his grief.

I grieved for the loss of my best friend, for the destruction of my idol. I grieved for the sometimes random malevolence of the Universe, for my inability to prevent irrational tragedy, for the uncertainty of life and relationship. I couldn't imagine ever turning against him. And I couldn't imagine why he had turned against me.

He grieved for something I could never fathom.

It was my mother's illness and ultimately her death that brought my father and me back together. I was eighteen. He was back in A.A. and was trying very sincerely to make amends. We were forced to converse to keep up to date about my mother's illness and her care. The day that he sat down to tell my sisters and me that our mother was going to die was the first time he and I had had an extended conversation in five years.

Slowly . . . gradually . . . we became friends again. And, eventually, over time, I gained trust in his resolve—this time he would stay sober. And without the influence of alcohol, he was the same wonderful person I had idolized in my childhood.

But it was hard, if not impossible, to pick up where we had left off. I had spent the majority of my teenage years psychologically living without a father. Now he was back, but something would forever be missing in me and in our relationship.

I remember meeting Elisabeth Kubler-Ross in 1976. More than anything else, I remember her saying, "Before we can see the Christ in ourselves, we have to see the Hitler." To this day it is one of the most powerful statements I have ever heard.

And my father and I had certainly seen the Hitler in ourselves. For years he caused me and the rest of the family only pain. After a certain point, instead of wishing for my old friend to return, I began to wish only pain and suffering for him.

There was even a time when I came close to murdering him. It was about five years after he had started drinking again. Our life had been a series of continuous battles . . . of screaming . . . rage . . and abuse.

One Saturday night he was in one of his frequent tirades and was humiliating and embarrassing my sister, who had brought a new boyfriend home for the first time. We were in the kitchen. My mother was preparing dinner. He ordered me to take off the boots I was wearing. Then he took one in his hand and threw it over his shoulder. It hit my mother in the head. I snapped. My blood boiled. I ran upstairs to my room. He followed me screaming out, "Don't you ever run away from me when I'm talking to you!"

Had he not followed me so closely and grabbed me when he did, had he left me for five more seconds to reach into the back of my closet and take hold of the Cuban machete he had given me several years earlier, I fully intended to try to split his head in half with it. Never before, or since, have I experienced such rage.

He grabbed me by the shoulder and wheeled me around. I immediately began pummeling his face with my fists. I wasn't a fighter and had certainly never struck my father before.

But since I hadn't been able to locate my weapon, I tried to do my best to kill him with my fists. I punched and smashed and punched and smashed and punched and smashed, lashing out with years of accumulated fury and hatred.

My mother ran into the room screaming and crying, pleading for us to stop. She collapsed in a heap on the floor, grasping her chest. My sister called the police and told them that my father was beating me.

When the police arrived, my father was contrite. He said he couldn't understand what they were doing in his house. They took him to the police station. He was placed on probation and had to make a few appearances before the municipal judge.

But what rips my heart open, even today, is that he never laid a finger on me. When I began pummeling him with my fists, he dropped his arms to his sides and just stood there taking every punch, like a condemned man surrendering to a lethal injection. He never raised a finger to defend himself, never ducked, never dodged a punch. He just stood there and let me hit him as long and as hard as I wanted to.

My mother didn't know that. My sister didn't know that. The police and the judge didn't know that. They all assumed that he was the aggressor.

And I allowed them to assume that. Because I thought that maybe, if he got arrested, and had to report to the judge, maybe if the whole town thought that he finally started beating his family, just maybe, he would clean up his life.

Nevertheless, I allowed him to be arrested on the basis of a mistruth. It's something I felt guilty about for decades.

So we had both seen the Hitler within us . . . quite clearly.

And it so frightened both of us that in the years following my mother's death, we worked very hard at trying to see the Christ within us. Each in our own way became intensely involved in spiritual pursuits. And much of our communication became focused on how we were doing in those pursuits.

It was an extraordinary healing and one for which I am profoundly grateful. Given the level of anger and hurt that had existed between us, it was remarkable that we were able to transcend it. We found many, many new ways to honor and appreciate each other. And we proved that, when love is the priority, there is no pain that cannot be healed.

Often it's really only pride and righteousness that encourage us to keep a wall up in a relationship. It's some distorted notion in our mind that tells us we must see to it that the offender suffers for his or her misdeeds. The ironic thing is that our habitual reaction merely perpetuates our own grief. Forgiveness is as much for our own healing as it is for the healing of the relationship. Perhaps more so.

My meeting in 1976 with Elisabeth Kubler-Ross had changed my life and inspired me to begin working with people who were terminally ill and people in grief.

Shortly thereafter, in early 1977, my father announced that his chronic hoarseness was caused by an "infection" in his throat that had to be removed, along with his larynx.

Reading between the lines I realized that what he called an "infection" must be malignant. I felt happy to have the new skills that Elisabeth had given me and I felt sure that he and I would work together and utilize them, to use his physical illness as a means of awakening spiritually and sharing an awesome, mysterious journey together.

But as it turned out, he wanted no part of that. His openness and spirituality began to fade. He had instinctively avoided doctors all his life and had been dabbling in Christian Science for a number of years. But when his illness came, he seemed to lose much of his faith, or at least much of what his faith was based on.

I wondered at times if his guilt about the years of drinking and abuse and his fifty years of smoking three packs of Camels a day had something to do with his resignation and despair.

He was one of those extraordinary individuals who have the ability to abuse their bodies and their surroundings for years and constantly bounce back. In spite of all he had done to himself, when he was 65 he looked like he was 45.

But his cancer diagnosis came when he was 72 and by then it had all begun to take a toll on him.

He became an interesting mixture of resignation and denial. At one level he seemed to surrender to his plight. At the same time he was fiercely determined to fight against the odds with every ounce of energy he had left.

But his approach became less and less "spiritual" and more focused on what the medical doctors recommended to forestall the inevitable suffering and death.

And he certainly didn't want to explore dying in an open and conscious way. Every time I tried to broach the subject, he would get up and walk out of the room . . . or fall asleep.

So I finally realized that he wasn't going to die his death the way I wanted him to. He was going to do it in his own way, with his own mixture of pride and dignity and what he understood to be courage. At times, I saw what he believed to be "courage" as stubborn denial of reality. But it was his death, not mine or anyone else's.

I ultimately found ways to support him in doing things his way.

Fortunately, circumstances allowed me to put my own life on hold in order to spend time with him. I became his cook, nurse, chauffeur, houseboy, companion, and advocate. I spent the winter months with him at his condo in Florida. I spent the spring, summer, and fall living near him in New Jersey and visiting with him nearly every day.

There were periods when for weeks on end I would drive him, every day, fifty miles round-trip to the hospital for radiation treatments. And when he became too weak to walk, we had to hire an ambulance service. The paramedics would come in to his apartment, move him from his bed to the gurney, and carry him out to the ambulance. I would ride with him to the hospital, sit with him for the hour and a half it took to get his treatment, and then ride back home with him.

But there was very little talk about what he was going through inwardly. Every time I tried to get that conversation going, he would stop it abruptly.

We watched television endlessly. When he felt well enough, we went out to restaurants. I just surrendered into his world and stopped as best I could all of my habitual resistance to it.

And I found a very interesting thing. After weeks and months of being with him, allowing him to be who he was, very occasionally he would allow a few moments of intimacy. I had surrendered into his world enough that he felt safe.

I remember sitting with him one evening on his terrace in Florida looking out at the water and the sunset. He was unusually quiet and was staring off into space. I finally asked him, "Dad, what are you thinking?" And he said, "I'm thinking that I'm going to be leaving you soon and I'm sad about that." I said, "I'm sad about it too."

And then, just as abruptly, he jumped up out of his chair and said, "Well, let's go watch the ballgame." I guess that was all the intimacy and honesty he could stand. And I realized that it had taken us our entire lifetimes to get to the point where we could have even that much.

I remember a time in the hospital when he had just gotten the results of a biopsy on a new tumor that had been discovered in his lung. As we had all expected, it was malignant as had been the "infection" in his throat a few years earlier.

We sat together in the family lounge on his floor. As I looked at the thin, feeble, frail, little old man in the chair, I thought about what he used to be. I saw the successful, hard-driving, upwardly mobile Republican businessman who always wore expensive suits and drove new Cadillacs, who always believed that "Nothing is worth worrying about for more than twenty minutes." He believed that the solution to all problems was to make more money.

But he had finally come up against a problem he couldn't buy his way out of. He had already consulted the best doctors money could buy. They all agreed . . . his case was hopeless.

So he sat staring at the floor. And now, instead of his once robust constitution, he was thin and haggard. Instead of an expensive suit, he wore an old bathrobe that was much too big for the size he had shrunk to. It was full of wrinkles and folds of excess material. It looked almost tattered. The bottoms of his silk pajama pants poked out under the hem of his robe and his pale, skinny, spindly legs poked out from under his pajamas. I wondered if his feet were cold as they sat loose and unsheathed inside the bedroom slippers that had also grown too big for his bony, tired feet.

Again, I took a deep breath and asked, "What are you thinking, Dad?"

He didn't look up. He didn't say anything. I began to assume that he wasn't going to answer me.

And then, he took the artificial larynx he now used to speak and slowly lifted it up to the droopy folds of skin in his throat. It made an odd buzzing sound that resembled a talking electric razor. Despite the strangeness, it was quite clearly my father speaking.

"I'm thinking how differently I would have lived my life if I had ever realized this was going to happen some day."

I said, "What do you mean, Dad? How would you have lived your life differently?" I could think of a lot of possible answers, but I couldn't figure out which one he would give.

"I would have done more things for other people," he said.

It was not what I expected. Because, despite his many years of drinking and carousing, he had always been a very generous person. And he had built a number of companies that employed hundreds of people and fed their families. I pointed all of that out to him.

But he was unimpressed by my recitation of his many virtues.

"No, no," he said with a hazy far-off gaze. "I always had a motive. I always wanted people to like me and to tell me how wonderful I was. I don't think I ever gave anything to anyone purely, just for the sake of giving."

I was startled and somewhat panicked by this revelation.

Startled because I had never known my father to take such a negative tone about himself. He had never allowed me, or anyone else for that matter, to see that there was a part of him that felt his failures as a human being outweighed his accomplishments as a businessman.

And I was panicked because as a grief counselor I despaired of the notion that my own father might die overcome with guilt.

He then said, "I wish there was a way to let people know that this is going to happen to them someday. I wish they could know because they might want to live their lives differently." Then he shrugged, "But they probably wouldn't believe it."

I began to realize that his grief was the by-product of his lifestyle and the things he had made his priorities. There was no way I could take it from him—it had become an integral part of his life. And I began to understand that to some degree, his surrender and resignation probably stemmed from his awareness that he needed to do penance. Not for me, not for my sisters, not for anyone else, just for himself.

And now, as I looked at the condition he was in, I realized that no matter what had happened between us, no matter how irrationally unkind he had been to me and the rest of the family when I was younger, I would have done almost anything I could to take away his suffering. To think back to the years when I wished suffering for him was agonizing. I wanted him to be at peace.

On top of all his other physical problems, he began to experience ministrokes and as a result his old alcohol-induced temper resurfaced. My sisters marveled at his ability to "shout" even though he no longer had a voice. He could still make them cower and run whenever he was in the middle of one of his frequent tirades.

At times he let us know, in no uncertain terms, what disappointments we were to him. I had known that for years, because he had always wanted a tall son who played basketball, attended Princeton University, and went to law school.

I, on the other hand was only 5'7", a terrible athlete, was interested primarily in music and theatre, and went to college in Florida.

Since my father sometimes couldn't remember their names, my sisters lived much of their lives feeling that they were mistakes on the way to a son.

I lived much of my life feeling that I was a mistake on the way to the "right" son.

One day he would say to me, "John, you're the finest son a man could have." The next day he would rail at me and shout, "When the hell are you going to get a job?!"

There were moments that pushed both of us to the edge of our models of what a father-son, parent-child relationship should be—and then, thankfully, they pushed us beyond. I remember especially the period when he suddenly began to lose control of his bodily functions. We were at his condo in Florida when one afternoon he completely lost control of his bowels and the entire bathroom was covered with his feces.

He was too weak to clean up the mess and had to ask for my help.

I was a little floored by the sight and smell of the pungent excrement everywhere I looked. But it's one of those moments in life when we automatically do what needs to be done, just because it needs to be done. No time to question, no one to call for help.

From that day forward, for the next two years until he died, he had to wear diapers. And I regularly cleaned him and changed him.

The first time, he was mortified. "This is horrible! No son should ever have to do this for his father!"

I quieted for a moment. And suddenly it occurred to me that we were living out a natural cycle. I said, "Gee, Dad, didn't you do this for me at one time?"

He was quiet for a moment. He thought back and smiled. "Yes, of course I did."

"Well," I said, "I'm just returning the favor."

And with that, all the awkwardness and revulsion melted away. We were sharing life as two human beings who, despite many difficulties, had found a way to be together in love.

I remembered that Ram Dass once wrote in a letter to grieving parents, "I can't assuage your pain with words, nor should I. For your pain is [your loved one's] legacy to you. Not that [he] or I would inflict such pain by choice, but there it is. And it must burn its purifying way to completion."

At times, the notion that pain can be purifying is difficult to swallow. But most of us, if we're really honest, know that, often, the most difficult periods of our lives have also been the most growthful.

Five long years after his original diagnosis, my father died at home in his own bedroom. I spent nearly an hour sitting at his bedside, holding his hand, cradling his head, touching his chest above his still, lifeless heart . . . talking to him and thanking him for all he gave me and taught me . . . encouraging him to go on and not to worry about us or his business.

When the time came, I helped the paramedics to lift his lifeless form onto the gurney so that they could remove him to the hospital morgue. In those moments it became clear to me that the being I had loved, and hated, and cared for, the being who had nurtured me, and taught me, and amazed me, and horrified me . . . who had inspired me and turned my world upside down, was not that body.

That day I felt a strange, inexplicable power and liberation. It was as if, at some level, my father's greatness had entered into me and his weaknesses were engraved on the screen of my consciousness forever. I could no longer see him as external to me. He was inside me. It was clear that we would have an ongoing relationship and that that relationship would exist within my own being. The withered bag of bones we loaded onto the gurney that day was like an old worn-out shirt . . . a dilapidated place where my father had once lived.

We conducted his funeral in a manner that attempted to bridge the gap between the dignity and tradition appropriate to my father's station in the community and my family's somewhat unorthodox views of the meaning of the rituals. But the real funeral took place for me privately in his bedroom just after he died. That was where I said "good-bye." That was where I said, "Thank you." That was where I said, "I love you."

That was where the rest of my life began.

Interestingly enough, about a year later, I fell into a severe depression. It was unusual because I had pretty much left depression behind after my teenage years.

But here it was again in all of its miserable glory. I couldn't shake it and I couldn't get a handle on it to understand its source. I knew that it had something to do with my father's death, but I also knew that as a result of my spiritual work and intuitive trust in the Universe, I wasn't depressed **because** he died. But I was very, very depressed, almost to the point of incapacity.

So I called Stephen Levine and told him all this. And when I told him that I didn't think I was depressed because my father died, he was quiet for a moment.

Then Stephen said, "No . . . Your father died a **long** time ago."

A chill went through me and a stabbing pain wracked my chest.

And, over the next days and weeks, as I reflected on what Stephen said, I began to realize that my "Daddy" had died when I was twelve—the first time I saw him drunk. And I had lived for twenty-two years with that grief *lurking inside me like some sinister parasite just waiting to emerge into full-blown illness. Suddenly I recognized that during all those intervening years, as long as his body was still alive, there was the possibility that that great gulf of grief could be healed. And now, without him around, my sub-conscious mind saw no possibility to right what was wrong.*

Then Stephen said to me something that has remained a cornerstone of my life and counseling to this day. He said, "Now you're going to have to father yourself. Now you're going to have to give yourself all of the love and support and compassion that you wanted from your father and never got."

In our grief we often look to blame other people, places, and events for conspiring to make us and our lives less than we wanted them to be. Much of my childhood was a nightmare, but I wouldn't trade where I am now for anything in the world. And everything that has happened previously in my life is what has led me to this place. So, in some sense, my father's alcoholism and insanity were among the greatest teachings of this lifetime—for both of us.

When we say youth is wasted on the young it's only because we realize later what precious opportunities were missed. But with the possible exception of having an adolescent body, there is really noth-ing that was available to us in our youth that isn't available to us now. All the freedom, exuberance, excitement, and spontaneity are just as available as our minds will allow them to be.

My friend Mark Victor Hansen loves to say, "It's never too late to have a happy childhood."

Much of grief is remorse over lost opportunities. In point of fact, the opportunities aren't lost; only some of the outlets for their expression. With creativity and insight we can recognize that rela-tionships can still be healed, love can still be experienced, and joy is ever-present.

One of the world's great religious traditions points out that at times we have to use a thorn to remove another thorn that has become embedded in our skin. At some level I think of my father as someone who offered himself up as a sacrificial lamb . . . to demonstrate through his own suffering what I *didn't* want to become.

It's also clear to me now that his suffering and the suffering it caused me were a blessing. I still love him immensely. I still hurt when I think of all we went through. I am grateful for the opportunity to care for him in his final years. And, from the "spiritual" perspective, I am overwhelmed by the great burdens he took on to tear my heart open.

More than anything, we need to remember that when our hearts are broken, they are also wide open. Our task is to fill the openness with love, awareness, and compassion . . . not to fill it with bitterness and self-pity.

Ultimately, it's our choice. And ultimately, the recognition must be that there is no payoff in spending our lives feeling victimized. This is a difficult school we've enrolled in. Some of the courses are harder than others, but each of them offers us the opportunity to learn to embrace life, and all of its confusing forms fully . . . openly . . . and lovingly.

Both of my father's "deaths" made me much of what I am today. I am eternally grateful to him and to the Universe that made us and brought us together.

Sometimes . . .
sadness is what moves us
to plumb our depths.
It is a very great teacher indeed.

Chapter Sixteen

"THE DEATH OF A CHILD"

"A LOVE SONG"

The mention of my child's name
may bring tears to my eyes
but it never fails to bring
music to my ears
If you really are my friend
please, don't keep me
from hearing the beautiful
music.
It soothes my broken heart
and fills my soul with love.
　　　　　　　- NANCY WILLIAMS

THERE IS ONE CERTAINTY ABOUT WHICH ALL GRIEF COUNSELORS SEEM to agree: *There is no pain greater than that of a parent who has lost a child.*

The death of a child appears to be out of the natural order of things. It seems inherently wrong.

And for the parent, there seems to be no way for the world to be "right" again.

The instinct to protect a child from danger is one of the most deeply ingrained elements of the human heart. Most parents don't even have to think about it. Most parents would lay down their lives without blinking an eye to protect their child's life.

But it's useful to recognize that our belief that the death of a child is out of the natural order of things is but one more facet of our uniquely "western" attitude toward death.

There are many societies in the world where parents have to give birth to *ten* children in order to have *one* who lives to the age of twelve. Most cultures haven't developed the medical infrastructure we have. Their children will fall victim to childhood diseases which we, for the most part, have either eradicated or controlled. And they will die from infections and injuries that could easily have been healed in our culture.

So the death of a child is not necessarily out of the "natural" order of things. Rather, in our modern western culture, we have defied, to some extent, the natural order of things. And we have become accustomed to that.

Now we are in an age where there are many new dangers to children created by the very advanced technological society that gave us cures to the "natural" diseases which, in an earlier time, threatened them. Now children are much more vulnerable to gun violence, both random and intentional. They are much more vulnerable to dying in automobile accidents. They are much more vulnerable to involvement with drugs and alcohol. They are much more vulnerable to the forms of cancer that arise from the environmental hazards created by our modern technological, industrial society.

And, amidst all the confusion and despair about life in our fast-paced, somewhat "values deprived" society, teenage suicide continues to rise.

In the summer of 1994, my wife, my mother-in-law, and I were on a visit to the southwest where we took a rafting trip through the Grand Canyon. After that, we drove up into Utah to Zion National Park.

The first morning we were there, the phone in our hotel room rang quite early. It was my sister, Judy, calling from New Jersey. She sounded upset.

She said, "John, there's no easy way to say this . . . Tim Lavery was in a very bad car accident last night. He was killed."

I was stunned. I felt like someone had hit me squarely in the stomach with a baseball bat.

Tim was our nephew, the eldest of our sister Carole's five children.

I loved him dearly. Although he was my nephew, he was thirty-eight years old, only five years younger than me.

Less than a month earlier he had visited our home in New Jersey with his mother. We had a wonderful week with him. He and I had always shared a great affinity, the two most radical and avant-garde members of an otherwise relatively conservative family.

He was an extraordinarily accomplished musician who was equally gifted playing classical, jazz, or rock. He had struggled in recent years with alcohol and drugs and had suffered through a series of complicated and fractured romances. He had married, had a child, and then divorced. Then he had a second child with a woman he didn't marry. Now he was trying to extricate himself from a relationship with a woman whose commitment to him wavered precariously. The uncertainty was keeping him in a painful state of discomfort and confusion. He was struggling to get his life together and came to visit us in order to get a break from his life back in Kansas.

When we were teenagers, Tim had looked up to me. He had followed me into rock music and many of the other trappings of the sixties. But when I left much of that behind for a more "spiritual" and academic life, Tim committed himself to being a musician. And he was great!

And, despite his struggles with romance and substance abuse, he was one of the kindest, most generous, most thoughtful human beings I have ever had the honor of knowing.

On the night of his death, he had been wrestling with his feelings for his latest romantic interest. She was being cold and dismissive. Although he had been sober for several weeks, that night he drank. He called her. Another man was at her house. Tim's heart broke. He ran to his car, jumped in, and drove off headed for a showdown at her house, engine roaring . . . tires screeching.

It was 1:00 a.m. on a rainy, foggy August night. He drove to Interstate 35 where, for some reason, he entered on the exit ramp and began driving north in the south-bound lanes. In a head-on collision with another car, he was thrown through the windshield. He died instantly.

Carole, his mother, was in bed at her home across town. She was awakened by the sound of sirens wailing on the nearby interstate. They gave her a strange, eerie, uncomfortable feeling.

At 2:00 a.m. her doorbell rang. It was the police. They told her that Tim had been involved in a "fatal" accident.

These are Carole's memories of the events that followed:

"I immediately went into shock. I was totally unable to cry. I couldn't remember what the word 'fatal' meant. I thought, Fatal? . . . Fatal? . . . **Fatal**? What does that mean?' I felt like someone had taken a knife and stuck it into my heart and then twisted it. I was totally unable to have any feelings. I was numb.

"I remember sitting and staring off into space saying, 'What will I do? What will I do?' I went into denial. I saw all of the policemen standing in my house in their uniforms and I knew that it was true, but I was totally unable to accept it.

"As a parent, I think you never get over the death of a child, because it's out of the order of things. You think you are supposed to go first. Your children are supposed to die after you.

"The two first emotions you have when you lose a child are shock and denial. And for the first year after Tim's death I stayed in that state. Even though I had to get up each day and go to work, everything I did was on autopilot. I didn't enjoy very much. I can't think of anything that was enjoyable to me.

"I found myself going to the cemetery almost daily. That's not something I naturally would do because, as a Christian, I don't believe that

that's where our loved ones are after they die. For me to do that was out of character. But it was an opportunity that was presented to me because my work caused me to travel right past the cemetery every day.

"I wondered why I had to do that. I believe now that the shock and denial are given to us by God to protect us from being totally devastated. They kept me from going so far down into depression and despair that I couldn't get out of bed and go to work each day.

"So my daily visits to the cemetery helped me to accept the reality of Tim's death . . . slowly . . . gradually . . . over time.

"I still felt horrible on the inside and I began to realize that it was going to take a lot of time for me to be able to truly accept Tim's death. Because Tim was so much fun . . . he was the child who stayed here in town . . . he gave me two precious grandchildren, and I just loved it when he would bring them over to my house. I just loved being with him. Tim made me laugh. He was fun.

"And he was very talented. I loved his music, and I just enjoyed his company. For me to lose that was the most terrible thing that had ever happened to me.

"I was just so disappointed. 'Disappointment' was the next emotion that came to me. Disappointment that he wasn't here. I had so many dreams for him. And I knew that he had so many dreams for himself.

"So I found myself in shock, in denial, trying to accept what had happened, and now having to deal with disappointment.

"I said, 'Lord, what am I going to do? I'm just a basket case.'

"I felt like someone who was trying to go downstairs when everybody else was coming up, and I was getting angry at the people who were in my way. For no reason at all, I was getting angry at all the people in my life.

"There were people who were totally inept at helping someone in a crisis. People would come up to me and say, 'Oh, I know exactly how you feel. I lost my dog' or 'I lost my cat.' 'I lost my mother,' or 'I lost a cousin.'

*"And everything inside me turned toward anger. I know what it is to lose a parent. And I know what it is to lose a dog or a cat. But **nothing** compares to losing a child. And unless you've gone through it, you are probably going to be inept at helping someone who is going through it.*

"So I would become very angry and agitated.

"Fortunately, there were some people who were really helpful. Some people knew exactly what to do and what to say.

"One of my friends would cry with me. When I would cry, she would cry, because her children had grown up with mine and we had been friends for years.

"Then there were special people who would come up to me and say, 'Carole, I can't imagine how you must feel. It has never happened to me. But I want to tell you something . . . I miss Tim. His music was a blessing to this community. His loss is a loss to the entire community.'

"And others would come up and tell me how much they missed him because he was always so kind and thoughtful, and he always took time to be friendly and helpful.

"Those are the things that minister to my heart and help me a great deal.

"So I'm going along in shock, denial, and disappointment and I'm having to go to work everyday. And Tim's band kept inviting me to come see them play. It took me two years to be able to do that, but I finally did. And I cried all the way through their performance. I hated it. I just hated it.

"I didn't hate the fact that those young men were still here and Tim wasn't. I just hated the fact that Tim wasn't.

"It took me two full years to begin to come out of denial and move back into reality and acceptance. Because, almost one year to the day after Tim's death, my mother died. And she had lived with me for many years.

"So, I'm ashamed to say it, but I went into self-pity. Self-pity overcame me after my mother's death when I realized that I was totally alone in my house.

"I turned to God and said, 'How did this happen? Why did this happen? I've devoted my life to you. I'm supposed to have 'life abundant.' I'm not supposed to have all these problems . . . or so I thought.

"But then I began to realize that no one had promised me a rose garden. Somehow, in my little Pollyanna-ish way, I thought that everything was always going to be okay. Even though I knew, intellectually, that that wasn't true, I think, in my heart, that's what I desired.

"So one of the things I think God wanted me to learn through all this was that growing up and maturing involves going through hard times. We can't be saved or protected from hard times. We have to go through them.

"I had to learn that this was a time in my life, a season, when I was walking through 'The Valley of the Shadow of Death.' I had to learn that I was walking through that valley, but I wasn't going to stay there. I had to learn how to walk through that valley, face my own mortality and that of my children, and learn to know God more than I did before.

"I don't believe you can get through these times without God. I don't believe you can get through these times without faith.

"So I can tell you that today, five years later, I can wake up in the morning and look outside and hear the birds and smile and I can celebrate Tim's life instead of feeling depressed and disappointed.

"I'm not saying that I'm totally over it. No. I never will be.

"I will **always** love him. I will **always** miss him.

"But I began to realize that I had to turn to God. I couldn't get up and face each day without turning to God.

"Several people have asked me, 'Have you heard from Tim?'

And I've said, "Oh goodness, no." I don't expect to hear directly from Tim. I'm not into that kind of thinking.

"But I had a dream one night, and I felt it was meant to help me . . . I was walking down this hallway with a whole bunch of doors, but there was only one open. I was a little scared to go through that door. I can't remember why. But my heart was racing.

"And I went through that door and there was Tim and he was kneeling down and just smiling from ear to ear. He was laughing out loud, just laughing. And he said, 'Mom, it's okay. Everything is okay.'

"And I was just elated. I remember wanting to hang on. I didn't want that dream to end. I wanted to just stay there and see him. It was over way too quickly. But it's helped me tremendously.

"Also, John, what you said to me, very early on . . . maybe a month after Tim died. You said, 'You have to remember, Carole, that what happened to Tim only happened once. You have kept replaying it over and over and over again in your mind. You've tortured yourself with it. But it only happened to Tim once. And it was over very quickly.'

"I tried really hard to listen to that. I tried really hard not to keep replaying it over and over again in my mind. But for the first few months, every night when I went to bed, I felt sick to my stomach. I couldn't sleep. And I kept seeing Tim, in my mind's eye, lying out on the highway by himself.

"I kept playing that scene over and over again in my mind's eye. But finally your words sank in and I was able to stop it when it would first start. I would say, 'No, you cannot do that to me . . . I won't receive it.' And I finally was able to not think about that anymore.

"I also had a period of great anger. I had a period of being angry with God . . . I questioned God, but more than that, I was angry with myself. I was angry with myself for what I didn't do as a mother. I was angry at myself for all the things that were wrong with me and my motherhood. I had to forgive myself, and that took a long time.

"Once when I was feeling anger at God, I 'heard' God say to me, 'Have you forgotten that Tim is not really dead? Do you think that I, the Creator of everything, would make a mistake? Do you think I would take Tim home before he was ready . . . or before he needed to be taken?'

"So then my anger at God melted into His sovereignty.

"And then I began the healing process. But I think I had to have the anger first. I think I had to go through the anger. The funny thing about it is that God already knows where we are.

"So finally I said to myself, 'If I'm ever going to come out of this, I'm going to have to move forward. I'm going to have to let the past be the past.'

"And during that time, I took all of the books on loss and bereavement that had been given to me by well-meaning friends and I threw them on the floor and kicked them across the room. Because I realized, finally, that there was a subtle way in which they were keeping me caught in the grief . . . they were keeping me caught in identifying myself as a 'bereaved person.' And I didn't want to spend the rest of my life as a 'bereaved person.' So I threw the books out.

"And gradually, over the years, with the help of my family and friends and God, I've moved through it. There was always someone I could turn to to say, 'I'm hurting today.'

"And often one of my other children would call and say, 'Mom, I'm

really missing Tim today, and I know how hard this must be for you. I just want you to know how much I love you, and how much I need you.'

"In order to be healed, we have to come out of our self-pity. We have to come out of our grief. We have to come out of our own little world and reach out to others. We have to start to help others. And that's what I started doing.

"But it took me a long time. My healing process is still going on.

"Now I think of Tim and I smile. Sometimes I still get choked up. Sometimes I'll be standing in the grocery store and someone will have something in their shopping cart that Tim really liked and the tears come. Sometimes I'll hear some beautiful piano music that I know he would love and the tears come.

"But I had to learn to concentrate on the things that were lovely about Tim . . . the things that were kind and pure about Tim. I had to think on the happy side, and realize that God had blessed me. For thirty-eight years, God had blessed me with Tim's life. And I had to thank Him and to celebrate the beauty that Tim was in my life.

"I had to focus my attention on the celebration of his life.

"But I had to go through all of these emotions. I had to come to terms within myself. It wasn't something that happened overnight. It was a slow process that happened day by day, hour by hour, minute by minute. I would have to say to God, 'You've got to help me. I'm miserable. It's bigger than me today. I need your help.'

"The biggest thing we have to do is to be honest—to admit where we are at from moment to moment. We have to know that we have great capacities and great potential and that we may never reach that potential unless we come to grips with ourselves and say, 'I'm feeling badly, and I don't want to feel this way.'

"We have to be honest. I may be very unforgiving of myself or someone who I know did something unkind to Tim. I had to work very, very hard to forgive the people who surrounded Tim. You've got to make the decision to let those feelings go. You've got to let them go or they will eat you alive. They'll kill you. They'll turn into bitterness and then you will be the only one who suffers.

"If I remain bitter about something, I'm the one who suffers. Then I can't be what I was meant to be.

"I think each of us knows deep down inside what our gift from God is. And I know that my gift from God is His joy. And I know that I have to give joy to others in order to receive it.

"I would still be in the bitterness if I hadn't started reaching out to others who were hurting. I made the transition by accepting the feelings I had as being normal and okay, and telling them to God, telling them to friends, voicing them, and in that process hearing them. And I knew that I couldn't stay that way, because then I would be of no use to my other four children, or anyone else. Ultimately, if I had stayed that way I would have been of no use to myself.

"And I would look at my grandchildren and they would look up at me with such love . . . I had to learn to get back the love that I had prior to Tim's death. I had to start giving that love again.

"It happened just an inch at a time. I started making the transition. And I woke up one morning and I was there.

"That doesn't mean that I've stopped missing Tim or that I've stopped longing to see him. I still have Tim's pictures all over the house, and I still listen to the tapes I have of his music . . .

"It just means that I've moved on.

*"The most important ingredient in healing grief is **love**."*

The Guest House
by Jelaluddin Rumi

This being human is a guest house.
Every morning a new arrival.

A joy, a depression, a meanness,
some momentary awareness comes
as an unexpected visitor.

Welcome and entertain them all!
Even if they're a crowd of sorrows,
who violently sweep your house
empty of its furniture,
still, treat each guest honorably.
He may be clearing you out
for some new delight.

The dark thought, the shame, the malice,
meet them at the door laughing,
and invite them in.

Be grateful for whoever comes,
because each has been sent
as a guide from beyond.

(Translation by Coleman Barks)

Chapter Seventeen

THE GIFTS WE GIVE OURSELVES TO HEAL

WHAT FOLLOWS IS A LIST OF RECOMMENDATIONS YOU CAN USE IF YOU are grieving. You can also share these with others who are working with a loss in their lives:

1. LET YOUR TEARS FEED YOUR HEART

Cry. Sob. Give yourself complete freedom to let your feelings surface.

Don't feel you have to be "strong."

There is no shame in crying. It is a natural, healthy reaction to the loss of someone we love.

Crying allows the body to discharge toxins . . . It facilitates the release of pent-up energy that might otherwise become destructive. It is the beginning of the healing process.

So feel free to let it all out, as often and with as much energy as you want. Find people to be around who aren't frightened by your pain and sadness. And don't be embarrassed by it.

It takes great strength to fully open to the natural feelings that are a part of this experience.

And if you have difficulty crying, don't worry. Just stay with the feelings.

If you feel too numb to cry, just relax and allow the feelings to surface slowly, moving through all this at the pace you intuitively feel comfortable with.

There is an old Native American saying which goes, *"The soul would have no rainbow if the eyes had no tears."*

The ability to feel the sadness will pave the way to feeling joy again.

Being fully human requires the ability, and the willingness, to experience both.

2. TELL YOUR STORY

You are going through a very traumatic experience. If it feels necessary and helpful to you, tell the story of what happened to as many people as you can, in as much detail as you want to.

Telling the story is another important part of the healing process. It helps you to integrate a difficult, incomprehensible reality into your life.

If your family and friends become uncomfortable with listening to the story, find others who are willing to listen. Find a bereavement group you can share with, or a bereavement counselor. Your funeral director, your cemetery, your church, or the local hospice are usually good resources for referrals to the people in your area who will welcome you and help you.

3. REMEMBER THE VALUE OF CEREMONY

No matter what the loss you are experiencing is, there is a significant healing to be gained from participating in a ritual, or ceremony that commemorates this extraordinary life transition.

Just as a wedding ceremony commemorates the marriage of two individuals, we need ceremonies to commemorate other "turning points" in our lives. Traditionally, when we are working with the death of a loved one, we hold a funeral. But many people in our modern culture question the value of a funeral. Instead of overlooking this important life event, design one that is meaningful to you. There are many innovative funeral directors in our culture today who are willing to help you find a personal, unique manner in which to honor your loved one's life and express your own grief. This is a very important step. Don't overlook it.

Similarly, when going through a divorce, or the loss of any other relationship, consider the possibility of a "divorce ceremony," a ritual of forgiveness and completion, an acknowledgment of the reality of the loss, and your commitment to begin the process of healing and growth. (Read *Embracing the Beloved* by Stephen and Ondrea Levine.)

4. OPEN TO THE POSSIBILITY THAT THE UNIVERSE IS PERFECT

The first step in helping ourselves to deal with grief and helping others to deal with grief is to open to the possibility that perhaps the Universe hasn't made a mistake . . . to give ourselves the gift of an open mind. To recognize that the torrent of thoughts, feelings, and emotions we experience in our grief can be the fuel that catapults us into a new and deeper connection with our own inner being, with the loved ones who are still in our lives, and ultimately with the loved ones who have died.

Next we recognize that our cultural conditioning has been to close our hearts when we experience "emotional overload." We've been taught that just when we are in the most pain, we must close off the only avenue we have at our disposal to help ourselves. How poignant! Perhaps no greater evidence exists that we have had it all backwards . . . that we would close our hearts just when we most need them to be open . . . that we would stop the flow of love just when we need it the most, when it's the *only* thing that will help us. And we don't even realize that we're doing it!

The result is that we become numb. We feel as if just beneath the surface lies this terrifying, raging, monstrous beast of feelings that will devour and obliterate us if we so much as let one claw out of the cage. We sit on our feelings like a gargoyle guarding the gates of Hell. We shove them down and shove them down because we're afraid that if we let them out they'll destroy us and overwhelm us. We're afraid that there's no way out!

The way out is the way through . . . to find the place in ourselves that watches the process like an impassive observer . . . to find that tiny little voice in us that sees everything we go through without judgment, sometimes with bemusement. It's that voice in us that wants to laugh just at the moment we are most angry; just when we are at the peak of an argument with our mate, it's the voice inside that giggles and says, "How ridiculous!" That's the voice with which we must become more familiar, which we must learn to trust. That's the part of ourselves that can see it all without panic.

The two most common immediate reactions to a significant loss are panic and numbness. Both arise out of fear . . . the fear that one's life will never be the same . . . the fear that one will never be safe . . . the fear that one will never experience love again . . . the fear that one *never has* experienced real love and that the only opportunity in this lifetime has been missed . . . the fear that one will remain forever with a sense of incompleteness because of the incompleteness of the relationship that has now been lost.

5. BECOME AWARE THAT NO RELATIONSHIP IS EVER LOST

Even if a person is physically absent from our lives, the memory of them and the awareness of the ways in which we would like to heal, change, or nurture that relationship stays very much alive within us. We need to connect with that aliveness within. We need to remember that person vividly. We need to bring them from time to time into the forefront of our consciousness. We need to fully experience all of the emotions their image awakens in us. Everyone we know and everyone we love exists in some form within us. They have become a part of us. We need to talk to ourselves and to talk to that person in the form they hold within us. We need to ask ourselves what we need to feel fulfilled in our relationship with that person. Then we begin to talk to our image of them, to move toward a resolution of any unfinished business. Maybe we just need to feel that we are still connected, that their physical absence has not ended the relationship. We need to realize that their physical absence has not ended the ability of that relationship to enhance or affect our life. Amazingly enough, we can carry that relationship within ourselves forever, and we have all the tools at our command to heal it and to resolve it, to nourish it, and to reach a real sense of completeness.

As it turns out, all relationship exists within our own beings anyway. We are conditioned to think that external people and conditions create us and create our emotional state. Our early childhood experiences shape the lens through which we see the world. And every relationship in our lives is conditioned by the needs, desires, and perceptions we bring to it. Remarkably, as we said earlier, when we "fall in love" what we are really doing is touching the place within ourselves where *we are love*. It's not that someone else has fed into us something we didn't have before we met them, they have merely awakened us to something that, for most of us, has been sleeping inside.

But we are conditioned to think that we can't have the experience without them and we panic whenever they leave our lives. We fear we've lost our ability to feel that rapturous, blissful feeling.

To heal our grief, we must know that love is a state of being within us. It is not given to us by someone else. We need to find a new way to access that place inside ourselves. That is the beginning of letting go of dependence. That is the beginning of the healing of grief.

6. CREATE A SACRED SPACE OF REMEMBRANCE

An extremely useful tool in this process is to create a special place in your home dedicated to the person who has died or left. A small table, a corner, one shelf on the bookcase—it's up to you. Place a picture or perhaps a few pictures of the loved one there. The pictures should represent the person in the form which is most dear to your heart, the one that most readily opens your heart and gets the feelings and memories flowing. You may want to place a candle nearby and perhaps bring some fresh flowers as an offering . . . maybe some incense.

If it feels comfortable to you, you may even begin to treat this place as an altar, a place of reverence and honor to the loved one. Then sit down in front of the photos and flowers and begin to breathe deeply in and out of the chest. Focus the breath on that area of the chest on and under the sternum where the physical heart resides. You might even imagine that there are two big nostrils in the center of your chest through which you are breathing. Begin to open to your loved one and allow any feelings which naturally arise to wash through your consciousness.

Feel free to talk to your loved one either silently or out loud. Talk to their picture or to the image you hold of them in your mind. Feel free to tell them what you are feeling, how much you miss them, how you wish things had been different, how much you love them. If there is a sense of anger at yourself or at them for the ways in which your relationship was unsatisfactory or merely for the fact that they are physically gone, feel free to tell them with all the passion and emotion you can muster. Keep talking until you feel you've had enough and then listen . . .

At some point, if you continue to do this exercise, you may begin to intuitively sense some resolution, or a shift in your relationship with your loved one. You may have some new understanding, some new perception, or a sense of completion. You will begin to understand the way in which relationships and loved ones stay within you and last forever. This is the beginning of the healing of grief.

You can keep doing the above exercises for weeks, months, or years. They may remain useful and vital or their usefulness to you may begin to fall away. It doesn't matter. Trust your own intuition about how long you need or want to do them.

7. Write a Letter to the Loved One Who Has Died or Left

This is another wonderful practice. Pour out your heart. Say everything you want to say, just as if they were able to hear it and receive it. If your letter is filled with loving thoughts, how wonderful. If it's filled with angry thoughts and despair, so be it. If it's a combination, no matter. Just pour out your heart fully. Make it as long as you want to. Use any language you want to. Feel free to say it all without guilt or remorse. If you have guilt or remorse, feel free to say that too. It's all fair game. Write as many letters as you like.

Do with this letter or letters whatever your intuition tells you is most useful. Put them on the altar you have dedicated to your loved one. Mail them to someone else. Tear them up and throw them away. Have a private ceremony and burn them. Leave them at the cemetery or in the mausoleum. Put them in a scrapbook or a display case. Put them under your loved one's pillow. Do whatever you instinctively feel will be most healing for you.

8. Keep a Journal

Every one of us is different. Some of us are geared to the spoken word. Some of us are more geared to the written word.

Whether or not you have ever kept a journal in the past, you may find that the regular, daily writing of your reflections on your experience will provide an invaluable outlet for your emotions and a creative and extremely effective tool for gaining understanding.

Sometimes it is useful to just sit down and start writing, with no particular goal in mind. Just write. Write whatever comes into your mind and heart. Don't edit. Just write. It's a process that's sometimes called "stream of consciousness." Feel free to jump from one thought to another. See new and unusual associations. Be totally honest . . . more honest than you've ever been. Say everything. Write about your fears . . . your anger . . . your judgment . . . your shame . . . write about your resentments and failures. Then write about what you need . . . write about the love, relationship, and forgiveness you are longing for. Don't judge what you write. Just let it all flow out like poetry. It's not intended to be published. It's only intended to be another outlet for your emotions and, possibly, a window through which you might access your intuition and higher wisdom.

Ultimately, you may or may not want to share your journal with others. But you may find it an extremely useful method of letting your sub-conscious mind plot out the route through your sadness. And you may gain a great deal of understanding about yourself and your experience that may not have come through any other means

9. FIND SAFE AND APPROPRIATE OUTLETS FOR YOUR ANGER

Almost inevitably, there is anger in some form connected with a profound loss. It is often the most difficult emotion for a grieving person to express or even acknowledge. Anger is the emotion that is numbed by drugs and alcohol. It is the emotion that is being hidden when you tell others, "I'm all right. Don't worry about me." You need to get it out, to express it in some way. Perhaps just talking will do it. Perhaps shouting will. Maybe punching a photograph of the loved one for whom you are grieving would actually be healing.

At her retreats, Elisabeth Kubler-Ross would recommend a plastic baseball bat and a pillow and would designate a special room where participants could go to safely vent their rage. It's interesting, because many of us are so uncomfortable with our own anger that we deny having it. We might say, "I don't need to do that." But amazingly often, just the initiating of a physical action which is expressive of anger is sufficient to unlock decades of repressed rage. We can often surprise ourselves when we recognize the volcanic intensity of emotion we have been sitting on for years. It lies there just beneath the surface of awareness and it needs to be set free like an angry caged animal. If we set it free, its power over us will diminish. If we don't set it free, we will never know what subtle, destructive damage it is doing in our lives. Extraordinary physical and emotional problems can arise as a result of repressed anger.

So go out and buy a plastic baseball bat and use it to beat on a pillow with all the explosive rage you can feel. Break old dishes. Pound the wall. Get it all out. Cry, scream, rant, and rave. This is an experience of being human. Feel free to let go of control and feel it all.

At the bottom of the anger, you may find a profound sadness. But you will understand that sadness much more fully after you have acknowledged and freed the anger.

10. FIND FORGIVENESS

After hours or days, weeks, months, or years—whenever it feels comfortable—begin the cleansing process of forgiveness. Sit down with the picture or the mental image of the loved one, breathe deeply, feel their presence, and begin to forgive them for everything they ever did, either intentionally or unintentionally, to hurt you, to disappoint you, to put you out of their heart. Forgive them for leaving. Forgive yourself for whatever you feel you did or didn't do or say that contributed to the sense of separation between you. Feel yourself moving back into their heart and feel them moving back into yours.

Then ask them for their forgiveness for anything you may have done, either intentionally or unintentionally, to hurt them, to disappoint them, to put them out of your heart. Feel them moving back into your heart and feel yourself moving back into theirs. Forgive all the misunderstandings, failed communications, and missed opportunities. Recognize that the human condition, by its very nature, contains a great deal of confusion. Forgive the abuse and neglect. Recognize that your relationship was a dance in which you didn't finish all the steps. Feel that you are now completing that dance with your partner off the stage. This part of the dance is your solo. You have each helped the other to grow and to deepen your compassion and understanding. That process can continue, and even be enhanced, now that the physical separation has given you the opportunity to tear down all of the psychological and emotional walls you constructed to stay separate even when you were together.

Perhaps it was your loved one who constructed most of the walls.

Perhaps it was you. It doesn't matter, because now you can both benefit greatly from the process of forgiveness.

11. LET GO OF YOUR GUILT

Begin to understand the way in which your guilt—about anything—reinforces your own sense of unworthiness. It keeps others out of your heart. It makes you feel you are unlovable. It is a major component of your grief. Begin to allow for the fact that all human beings are filled with confusion and all human beings make mistakes. If your relationship with someone else has made you aware of parts of your personality you'd like to change, be thankful. At one level you may have let yourself and someone you love down. At another level, they have given you the opportunity to see something in yourself that you'd like to change. Maybe you never saw it before, or maybe you never saw it so clearly. Be thankful. Our loved ones are our teachers. Sometimes they show us, by example, what we want to be. Sometimes they show us what we don't want to be. These insights are their gifts to us. They are part of their legacy. Again, ask their forgiveness, ask your own forgiveness, and go on . . .

There's an old saying in the Sikh religion that goes, *"Once you know God knows everything, you're free."*

Once you know God knows everything, you're free. How amazing! And Alcoholics Anonymous has been telling us for years, "You're only as sick as your secrets."

Much of what we are guilty about are things that no one else knows about us—our secrets. We have walled off another corner of our hearts with private thoughts and convictions about things we have said, thought, or done that we feel are unforgivable and define us as essentially unworthy, sick, depraved, and hopeless wretches.

At some point in our lives, we all need to have someone—a close friend, a counselor, a spiritual teacher, a confidant—to whom we can express everything we have kept buried inside, secure in the knowledge that this person will hear it all in a spacious, loving awareness without judgment and without misusing what they know.

For many of us, our minds have become like cesspools of psycho-logical excrement we refuse to allow to come to the surface. Somehow, we need to bring it all into daylight. We need to know that *every one of us has a secret stash* of shame, embarrassment, and remorse. And we need to know that we are still capable of giving and receiving extraordinary love, in spite of it all. We need to feel the freedom of knowing that God knows everything.

12. WORK WITH YOUR ANGER AT GOD, OR THE UNIVERSE

Acknowledge and then let go of your anger at God. This is a dif-ficult one. It involves all kinds of horrific self-judgments and guilt. But in point of fact, at some level *whenever* we are angry about any-thing, we are really angry at God. We are really saying, "If I were God, I wouldn't have put me in this situation. If I were God, I wouldn't have allowed my loved one to die. If I were God, I wouldn't have allowed this divorce. If I were God, I wouldn't have created a jerk like this who would upset me and be unreasonable. If I were God . . ." It's all part of assuming that the Universe is filled with mistakes. But maybe, just maybe, there's a perfection to it all. A large part of grief is the sense of separateness and isolation, the terrible feeling that we are alone in an alien and malevolent world, the feeling that we have no connection to this vast, mysterious, seemingly uncaring Universe. It's a state of being that is sometimes known as "the dark night of the soul." How many times, though, have we heard people say that the most difficult experiences of their lives have been the most growth-ful?

From a certain perspective, there is an observable order in the Universe. It's clear that God, or whatever we want to call the creative force behind it all, can handle and can forgive all of our peculiar human foibles. Acknowledge that you are angry, feel it fully, and then visualize the anger as a tangible thing, like a pile of red-hot angry words or hot coals. Imagine that you are placing your pile of anger on a beautiful silver platter and then give it away. Get rid of it. Let the Universe consume and digest it. Ask God to take it. It's okay.

Human minds churn out all kinds of irrational, bizarre, and hostile thoughts. Your thoughts aren't you. They're just your thoughts. They come and go in an irrational, unending stream. Just watch them with dispassion and let them go. We all have thoughts that embarrass and horrify us. But those thoughts, so long as we don't act on them, do not touch the core of our beings, our souls. The guilt about thoughts is much more damaging than the thoughts themselves.

13. INCORPORATE MEDITATION, CONTEMPLATION, AND PRAYER INTO YOUR DAILY LIFE

In order to help quiet the "screaming trumpets" of rage, grief, horror, despair, and anger in your mind, consider learning and practicing some form of meditation. Many techniques don't require any particular religious or theological beliefs. They only require you to believe that you would benefit from a more peaceful mind. And most of these practices can be a wonderful enhancement to your spiritual path.

Dr. Dean Ornish, whose pioneering work on the relationship between diet, exercise, mental and emotional health, and disease has won him great respect and recognition in recent years, says, *"I have never found anything as powerful as **meditation**."*

A great teacher of meditation once said that the human mind, left to its own devices, "carries on like a drunken monkey with St. Vitus Dance that's been stung by a scorpion." In other words, it's completely out of control.

> *The human mind is an exquisite servant but a terrible master. You need only observe what your mind has been doing in your grief . . . how it obsesses about certain things, seemingly beyond your control . . . how it jumps from one troublesome thought to another.*

One of the major highways through grief is quieting the mind and loosening the belief that our thoughts are who and what we are. They are not. They are just our thoughts. Part of our grief is that we are much larger and more dynamic beings than our thoughts usually allow us to be.

Meditation helps by calming our metabolism, lowering our heart rate and blood pressure, and contributing to good health in any number of other ways.

An important byproduct of the practice of meditation can also be the development of a clear sense of what it is in ourselves—and therefore in others—which transcends our physical form.

Dr. Larry Dossey, in his book *Prayer is Good Medicine* cites innumerable scientific studies which clearly indicate the positive effects of prayer on one's physical and emotional health. When people pray, and are "prayed for," they show marked and measurably enhanced improvement over other people—with the same condition—who do not utilize prayer.

And it can be extremely helpful, if you don't already have one, to form an affiliation with a church, or temple, or community of like-minded spiritual seekers.

> *Our spiritual family can be an invaluable source of love, caring support, and insight into the deeper meaning of our life experiences.*

But it is extremely important that the spiritual community is one that is in harmony with your inner conviction and awareness. There is nothing more supportive than a spiritual community that feels like "home."

Conversely, there are few things as painful as trying to fit into a spiritual community with which one doesn't feel in harmony.

Trust your own "inner guidance" about all these issues.

14. Be More Mindful of Your Own Physical Health

Don't neglect your own body. Take extra care to feed it nutritious and appetizing foods. Try to steer away from junk foods, fat, sugar, alcohol, and caffeine. These substances all have negative effects on our metabolism and our minds.

In a spirit of caring for and nourishing yourself, get involved in a weight-loss or purification program you have been long neglecting. Go out and buy Dr. Andrew Weil's *Eight Weeks To Optimum Health* and get your body and your spirit on the road to a new life.

On the other hand, if you feel that eating a huge banana split will bring you joy, by all means run out and get one, or two, or three! Eat it without guilt. Give yourself permission to have pleasure.

Try to get a lot of sleep. It's very healing. And try to get a good amount of exercise. You might learn and practice *yoga*, or some other form of contemplative movement such as *tai chi* or *chi quong*. These are extraordinary methods for releasing physical tension and facilitating the free flow of physical energies.

Walk, run, bicycle, hike, swim. Go to beautiful places where you can be alone and quiet in natural surroundings. Sit by a river, or on the beach. Walk in the forest. Hug a tree! Tune to the rhythms of nature. Begin to hear the reassuring wisdom behind it all. Recognize that what makes the grass, trees, and flowers grow is exactly the same thing that is inside of you growing your cells, your hair, beating your heart, enlivening your consciousness.

If you have the time and financial freedom, spend days at a local spa being pampered with massage and healing energy. Travel and see new horizons. Visit old friends and family members in other areas of the state or country. Take this as an opportunity to explore possibilities in life that you avoided or neglected during the course of the relationship.

Also, seek out other human beings who feel "comfortable" to you—people with whom you can share at all different levels of your life. And seek out opportunities to give and receive affection. Visit nursing homes, veterans hospitals, and day care facilities. Hold hands, comfort babies, give others warm affectionate hugs. Now that you have experienced the devastation of loneliness and disappointment, you can be a deep, compassionate heart to help others heal.

Few things in this life are as healing as giving and receiving affectionate physical contact with other human beings. I'm not necessarily talking about sexual contact. Any sort of loving touch will go a long way toward helping you overcome your sense of isolation and aloneness. Take advantage of the opportunities. Life is short and uncertain.

15. BE CREATIVE

Anything you can do that helps to "create" can be extremely healing.

Caroline Myss, in her wonderful book, *Anatomy of the Spirit*, recommends, among other things, gardening. The simple act of planting flowers, fruits, or vegetables, and tending them with nurturance and love helps to tune us to the ongoing cycles of nature . . . to help us feel "connected" . . . to facilitate the transition to a new life.

Caroline talks about a mother whose husband was killed in a car accident. Each day the mother would perform some small task that represented her intention to rebuild her life, working consciously to bring her life into the present. She planted flowers which represented new life. And with each flower she planted she would say, "I'm planting a new beginning for myself and my children."

The same woman also was working with a cervical cyst, and each time she weeded her garden, she would feel the process symbolically representing the "pulling" of the cyst from her body. The cyst eventually dissolved on its own.

There are infinite other possibilities to be creative . . . painting, sculpting, or some other form of graphic art . . . learning to play a musical instrument, singing, joining a local theatre company, painting the house, redecorating the house, writing poetry, writing a novel, writing your autobiography . . . volunteering in nursing homes or day care centers . . . helping others. There may be many things you wanted to do that the relationship inhibited in some way. Now you are free to learn, explore, and expand in ways you have only dreamed about.

16. CONSIDER PROFESSIONAL THERAPY OR COUNSELING

By all means, if your grief feels overwhelming, seek professional help. There are many, many therapists now specializing in grief therapy and many, many groups and workshops available. There is no shame in asking for some outside guidance to steer you through the maze of your own thoughts and emotions. And, often, even just a few sessions can help to "re-direct" you and begin to loosen the quagmire of fear, loneliness, anger, despair, and confusing, troublesome thoughts.

Most of us have, at one time or another in our lives, felt that we were incapable of integrating our own psychological experiences. Our society is full of people who can help at those moments. Some will take your hand and lead, others will just point you in the right direction. Trust your intuition to tell you what you need and what you feel comfortable with.

Very often, even a few sessions with a skilled counselor can make a profound difference in your outlook and your state of mind.

17. LAUGH

We all know that there are times in life when, no matter how hard we try not to, no matter how inappropriate we may think it is, we burst forth in laughter. It is a tremendously healing release of pent-up energy.

And although despair, at times, may foster a mind-state in which we feel we don't want to laugh, there is seldom anything that would be more helpful.

Often, we hear a lot of laughter at funerals. Some of it may be overly giddy, bordering on hysteria, but it provides an appropriate balance to the otherwise somber solemnity that was, for decades, expected at funerals.

Many of our loved ones were fun loving and jovial during their lives and would probably be distressed to think that their humor was forgotten in the face of their physical death. How many people, when asked what they would like their funeral to be, have suggested some sort of party where their family and friends could have good food and fun?

Norman Cousins, in his monumental book, *Anatomy of an Illness*, described in detail how he cured himself of a disease his doctors had characterized as both incurable and terminal. His prescription: *laughter.*

He had a movie projector sent to his hospital room and had endless supplies of funny movies delivered. He spent hours each day watching films of Allen Funt's "Candid Camera," the Marx Brothers, Laurel and Hardy, and other great comedians of our time, howling with laughter.

Over the course of a number of months, his disease went into remission. He was, essentially, cured by weaving his "laugh therapy" together with skilled medical intervention in a unique partnership.

In another wonderful book, *Head First*, Norman further explains his refreshing and insightful theories and experiences of healing.

On the other hand, I have heard a number of people who, faced with cancer, their own or that of a loved one, say, "There is nothing funny about this disease," or "There is nothing funny about death."

Humor at life's most profound and difficult moments must be handled delicately and with sensitivity. It must honor the emotional needs and sensitivities of everyone involved. And there are times when it is simply not appropriate.

My good friend Allen Klein has written a number of books on the effectiveness of laughter as a tool for healing grief and developing the sensitivity to use it wisely and compassionately. I highly recommend you read his book, *The Courage To Laugh*, in order to look into this important subject more deeply.

Allen's own experience of grief following his wife's death and the subsequent help he received from comedy and laughter represented a major turning point in his life. He is now a much sought-after speaker and is regarded as one of our nation's foremost authorities on using humor as an aid during life's difficult times.

18. RELAX AND TAKE YOUR TIME

Don't feel that there is any rush. Our society always wants us to "feel better fast." If you want to work with grief in a way that will be truly enlightening, that will have a lasting effect, that will integrate into your experience in a meaningful way, it will take time.

In a very real sense, grief never ends. We merely learn how to incorporate it into the totality of our beings rather than pushing it away. When we can embrace *all* of the aspects of human life, the joys and the sorrows, we no longer fear that we will drown in sadness. But we must be willing to feel it. It's part of the curriculum we're taking. The unwillingness to feel is what drowns us.

So it may take weeks, months, or years. And fifty years from now we may still cry because the human side of us misses having a loved one physically present. But we are not our bodies, and our relationships don't exist in our bodies—they exist in our heart, in our mind, in our soul. When we become aware of that reality, we begin to loosen the grip of grief.

The cruelest thing we can do to someone in grief is to suggest that they should be "getting over it" within some pre-determined time span. A mother who has lost a child *never* gets over it. She will, hopefully, go on with life, love more deeply, feel grateful for the time she did have with that child, become more consciously attuned to her other children, if she has any. But she will never "get over it." The pain is the child's legacy to the parent. Hopefully, the parent can use the pain as a lever to pry open whatever doors in the heart have been closed.

Grief is a part of human life. We don't get over it. We can, however, use it as a tool to grow, to improve our relationships, to remind us to stay present in this moment, to experience the expansiveness and radiance of our beings, who and what we really are, and the truth that grief is only a portion of who we are. We can fully and consciously confront our grief and at the same time laugh, love, rejoice, and live our lives with energy, conviction, and enthusiasm. Grief is a problem in our society only because we are so afraid of it.

19. EXERCISE: THE BREATH THAT HEALS

One of the most healing methods of working through grief is the practice of breathing into the heartspace in the center of the chest.

Take some time each and every day to do the following: Close your eyes and bring your awareness to the place in your chest where your heart resides. Breathe deeply in and out of that center, imagining that you have a large opening where your sternum (the solid bone in the center of the ribcage that protects the heart) is located.

Take several deep, long, slow, relaxed breaths and imagine that you can feel the air gently moving through that opening like a warm reassuring breeze.

Then gently imagine a warm, light-filled, candlelit room in the center of your chest. All of your loved ones reside within that room. Imagine each of them in the form that is most dear to your heart, the one that makes you feel the most love. Take time to visualize each one, working primarily with the ones you miss the most. See and feel their presence there. Know that they are always with you. Know that you can always talk to them, ask their advice, laugh with them. This is not living in the past . . . it is the recognition that our love is always alive. It is most alive in this present moment.

Ask your loved ones for their guidance. Ask them to help you overcome your loneliness.

And remember,
your loved ones are
always with you,
eternally alive
in the warm, soft womb of your heart
You are not alone . . .

Chapter Eighteen

PREPARING FOR OUR OWN DEATH

> Morrie said, "Everyone knows they're going to die, but nobody believes it . . . If we did, we would do things differently."
>
> "So we kid ourselves about death," I said.
>
> "Yes. But there's a better approach. To know you're going to die, and to be prepared for it at any time. That's better. That way you can be more involved in your life while you're living."
>
> "How can you ever be prepared to die?"
>
> "Do what the Buddhists do. Every day, have a little bird on your shoulder that asks, 'Is today the day? Am I ready? Am I doing all I need to do? Am I being the person I want to be? . . . The truth is . . . once you learn how to die, you learn how to live."
>
> MORRIE SCHWARTZ IN *TUESDAYS WITH MORRIE*
> BY MITCH ALBOM

IN HIS WONDERFUL BOOK, *TUESDAYS WITH MORRIE*, MITCH ALBOM recounts his weekly visits with his old college professor, Morrie

Schwartz, as Morrie slowly died of ALS (Lou Gehrig's Disease). Their conversations are extraordinary . . . inspirational . . . heart warming . . . visionary insights into the most profoundly simple Truths of human existence.

When I first read *Tuesdays with Morrie,* I was reminded of the time I spent with my father as he slowly came face to face with his mortality. I especially remembered the day when we sat together in the hospital and he said, *"I'm thinking how differently I would have lived my life if I had ever realized this was going to happen some day."*

When I asked him how he would have lived his life differently, he said, *"I would have done more things for other people."*

As I looked at him that day, I recognized the poignancy of our predicament. *How much of life is missed when we ignore the inevitability of death!*

As we discussed in Chapter Seven, many other societies have seen all of life as a preparation for death. But our death-denying culture has seen all of life as an opportunity to pretend that death is not a reality, that no preparation is necessary, that if we banish the subject from polite conversation, and we cover-up all evidence of death, our lives will be happier.

But there is so much evidence to the contrary. In nearly every interaction I have had with people who are dying and people who are grieving, those involved have expressed the fervent wish that they had somehow known sooner . . . that they had had the opportunity to prepare.

And so many people who are dying have said that they have *"never felt as alive"* as they do since they found out they are dying.

There is a wonderful old story of a Buddhist master who gave intricate teachings on the quality of *impermanence* in the Universe. The master had been given the gift of a beautiful crystal goblet from which he drank his water. The master was asked, "If everything is impermanent, how do you enjoy life? How do you enjoy that fragile, delicate crystal goblet?" The master replied, "It's very simple, you see. For me the glass is already broken. I drink from it. I enjoy its beauty. I delight in seeing the rainbows it creates when the sunlight streams through it. But it's already broken. Someday when a wind blows it off the shelf, or I carelessly knock it off the table with my elbow, all I need to say is, 'Ah, so . . . ' because it's already broken."

In that sense, everything in our life is already broken . . . and everyone in our life is already dead.

Many cultures have given their people reminders . . . some may seem gruesome to our squeamish sensibilities: A tribe in Africa presents each member with their own burial shroud when they pass into adolescence. They wear it over their left shoulder every day for the rest of their lives. It is not used for warmth, or decoration, only to wrap their body at the time of their death . . . it is a reminder . . . a reminder to be *awake* . . . to live their lives *fully, consciously, compassionately, honestly* . . . every day. The Native American Hopi tribe gives their young a "death chant" as they pass into adolescence . . . it's a phrase they are taught to repeat every day, especially at moments of danger and uncertainty . . . it is intended to assist them in merging with "The Great Spirit" when they do die. Tibetan Buddhist monks use the tops of human skulls as food and drink containers . . . they are reminded—as they enjoy *their* food and drink—that their food and drink are contained in a body part of someone who also, previously, "enjoyed" their own food and drink. A monk in Rome artistically and meticulously decorated the inner chambers of a church with the skeletal remains of thousands of monks who died before him. It's an extraordinary sight to behold. And monks in various traditions around the world spend long hours in cemeteries meditating on the meaning of life.

But our culture has few, if any, tools that are intended to remind us of our mortality. The sometimes overwhelming grief we experience in the wake of loss comes because we are unprepared . . . we never thought about it . . . we pretended it wasn't a possibility.

*There is one simple thing wrong with you . . . you think you
have plenty of time. You think your life is going to last forever
. . . whatever you're doing now may be your last act on earth
. . . There is no power that can guarantee that you are going to
live one more minute . . . There's a strange consuming happiness in acting with the full knowledge that whatever one is doing
may very well be one's last act on earth. I recommend that you
reconsider your life and bring your acts into that light.*

DON JUAN IN *JOURNEY TO IXTLAN*
BY CARLOS CASTENEDA

So how do we begin to prepare?

There are a number of meditative and yogic practices which
involve the visualization of one's death . . . They can be extremely
useful.

But one of the most effective ways I know in this society is to conscientiously make all of the legal arrangements many of us have
superstitiously postponed:

Draw up a will with a qualified attorney, and make it a binding
legal document. Assess what kind of life insurance requirements you
have and sit down with a reputable insurance agent to make sure you
are properly covered.

And, as we discussed in Chapter Nine, one of the most effective
methods I know of is to plan our own funerals.

Sit down with your family and loved ones and openly discuss what
you would like and what they would like. There are many people
nowadays who feel that a funeral is unnecessary. But much psychological research suggests otherwise.

Ritual performs an important function in human life, especially
at times of significant transition. It is extremely useful to have a ceremony that commemorates the life of someone you love . . . that
honors and reviews that life. And funerals are intended to help family members bring closure . . . to help them fully recognize the reali-

ty of the physical death so that the next phase of relationship with that person can begin.

Most modern, reputable funeral homes and cemeteries are equipped to meet with you and your family, to discuss the many options available, to make the arrangements, and even to help you finance the costs of a pre-planned funeral over time. Financing is not usually available to families when a funeral is not pre-planned.

Feel free to be creative. Design your own rituals . . . design unique ceremonies. Let your imagination run free. Let your family members' imaginations run free. Create rituals and ceremonies that will be inspirational, moving, meaningful, and healing . . . perhaps they might even be fun.

Some family members may find it difficult to start the conversation. But this is a very, very useful exercise. It may be the first time you have all really sat down together, looked in each other's eyes, and realized that you will not all be together forever . . . there will come a time when someone in the room is gone . . . and then another . . . and then another . . . and so on. You may even want to have a "rehearsal." Imagine how meaningful it would be to have each family member play the role of being laid out in a funeral home while the other family members surround the "deceased" and discuss their emotions, talk about how much they "loved" that person, and what they wish they had done differently.

Making plans for your funerals can bring that reality home. And, in actuality, what a precious gift! What a beautiful opportunity!

Not only does the planning and arranging of your funeral relieve your family of a major economic burden at the time of your death, but it also relieves them of an added psychological burden.

Let your relationships open and flourish in the awareness that our ability to be together in physical form does not last forever.

Let your life open and flourish in the knowledge that every day could be your last . . . or the last for someone you love.

Use this awareness to make the most of every precious day on earth.

Chapter Nineteen

WORKING WITH OTHERS WHO ARE DYING AND GRIEVING

Real happiness . . .
Lies in making others happy.
— MEHER BABA

AT THE AGE OF TWENTY-TWO, I WAS NEARING THE END OF MY UNDER-graduate work at the University of South Florida and I was dealing with a crisis common to many adolescents and people in their early twenties. I felt my life was meaningless.

I was in Berkeley, California visiting my good friend, Dr. Allan Y. Cohen. Allan is an extremely skilled psychotherapist. One morning I decided to tell him what I was struggling with. I said, "Allan, my life is meaningless."

By that point in our friendship, Allan knew me pretty well. He was very familiar with the circumstances of my life. He looked humorously bewildered and stunned. Incredulous, he said, "John, what on earth are you talking about?"

I repeated my dilemma as if he hadn't heard me the first time. "Allan, my life is meaningless."

"Oh!" he said smiling, his deep brown eyes dancing with delight. "Is that all? There's a simple prescription for that! *Whenever you feel your life is meaningless, start doing more things for other people!*"

When I run workshops for the employees of hospitals, nursing homes, hospices, cemeteries, and funeral homes, the question I am most frequently asked by people who have only been on the job a short time is, "How do I avoid saying or doing something that will make a person cry?"

The answer is simple and two-fold:

1. *You can't avoid it.*

And,

2. *If you provide an environment in which they feel safe enough to cry, you have done them a great service.*

As we said earlier, the process is very much akin to being a lifeguard. It's impossible to save someone who is drowning unless you, yourself, are a strong swimmer.

And it is impossible to work effectively with people who are dying and/or grieving unless you have done some serious work on integrating the losses in your own life.

Your willingness to read this book may be the first step along that path. Or it may be one of many.

No matter, you have begun the process. Remember that the teacher can only take the student as far as she or he has gone. As Ram Dass has so often said, *"The only thing you have to give another being is your own being."*

It's not what you are or what you know. It's *who you are*. It's your state of awareness. It's what you *communicate* both verbally and nonverbally when you walk in the room. In working with grief, it's the degree to which you can make someone else *feel* your *love . . . acceptance . . . wisdom . . .* and *inner peace*.

So working with others becomes work on yourself, because if you aren't loving, if you're not accepting, if you haven't cultivated wisdom and inner peace, then there isn't a lot you can offer. Your work on yourself will give others the opportunity to move through and integrate their own sadness to whatever degree you have moved through and integrated yours.

From that standpoint, everything you encounter that frightens you, angers you, or leaves you in distress, is a *gift*. It is a gift from the Universe to show you where you are clinging to models of how things *should be* rather than *how they are*.

In the beginner's mind there are many possibilities.
In the expert's mind there are few.

SHUNRYU SUZUKI
IN *ZEN MIND, BEGINNERS MIND*

A. LEARNING THE BASICS

Seeing People Who Are Dying and Grieving as Teachers

This is one of the most important teachings Elisabeth Kubler-Ross gave us. It is the principle that we allow the people we serve and counsel to *teach us* what their experience is, rather than formulating some system, format, or set of ideals with which we seek to teach them.

It is what Shunryu Suzuki called "Beginner's Mind."

It is cultivating the ability to walk into a room with someone who is grieving or dying without a preconceived notion of what *should* occur, what *should* be said, or what they *should* be feeling.

It is setting aside the idea of being an "expert"—there are *no experts* in this work.

The most useful image is to see ourselves walking by their sides rather than leading them.

Each person who dies and each person who grieves does it uniquely, individually. What experience could possibly be more personal?

So there is no way to apply systems, rules, or emotional roadmaps.

Our job is to be a presence, rather than a savior.

A companion, rather than a leader.

A friend, rather than a teacher.

There is a wise old saying that goes, "God gave us two ears and one mouth for a reason: We should *listen* twice as much as we talk."

> *The five most powerful words*
> *for someone in grief to hear —*
> The simple phrase:
> *"I'm right here with you."*

One of the most devastating aspects of any grief, no matter what the cause, is the sense of isolation and aloneness. It is amplified by the sense that there is no one who is really willing to share the pain and sadness.

If you can communicate to someone in the midst of devastating grief, either on the phone or in person, that you are willing to be present with them, right now, in this moment, to witness and hold all of their pain and sadness, that your heart is open to them and that you will not turn away or change the subject or rush them along no matter how difficult what they are going through becomes, you will have communicated *real concern* and a real commitment to help them. It can be extremely difficult work. But it is extraordinarily fulfilling work.

Stephen Levine in his wonderful book *Who Dies?* deals with this issue very clearly.

People approaching their own death and people in grief are extremely sensitive to the most subtle nuances of communication. They are usually acutely aware when others are "turned off," or frightened, or uncomfortable about their predicament and will usually modify their communication accordingly. They listen intently to each word or phrase that is said and can easily misinterpret something that is not communicated with clarity. As a result, they find fewer and fewer outlets where they can express their grief and fewer and fewer opportunities to begin or continue the healing process.

In workshops for grieving people, I usually ask two questions:

1. *"For how many people is this experience the most difficult thing you have ever gone through?"*

Usually about 75-80 percent of the people raise their hands.

Then I ask,

2. *"How many of you have felt very alone during this experience and have sensed that your sadness is 'too much' for the people around you to handle?"*

About 95 percent of the people raise their hands.

So they become desperate and begin to look for other people or places outside their family and friends where they can get help. Or they turn within. There they either attempt to live in isolation with a private pain that seems unbearable and unresolvable or they search for some way to numb the pain.

The greatest gift you can give them is the feeling that you are with them, that you won't abandon them, and that your heart can hold the devastating sadness they feel.

B. ALLOW THEM TO TELL THEIR STORY

Have you noticed that when people tell the story of a devastating loss they will often begin by announcing the date and time it happened, or it began, or they got the news? They say, "On November 24, 1972, at 1:34 in the afternoon . . ." That is the moment their life changed forever. That is the beginning of their story. It is most important that they find someone to whom they can safely and comfortably tell their story, many, many times over, if necessary.

One of the most important healing ingredients of the twelve-step treatment programs that have evolved out of Alcoholics Anonymous is that they provide an environment where people can continue to tell "their story" safely, without being judged, for years if necessary. That is how the mind learns to come to grips with devastating, incomprehensible, and unacceptable experience.

But people in grief are often met by friends and family who say, "Look, I've heard the story! How many times are you going to tell me the same thing?" Or, "Can't we talk about something more pleasant?" Or, "Don't let your mind dwell on such negativity, dear . . . Let's go shopping."

So real communication and true connection are lost. And the phone stops ringing, the doorbell stops ringing, and people are left isolated because their friends and loved ones just can't handle it and no longer feel comfortable being in their presence.

Remember also that when someone in grief feels safe enough to tell you their story, it is not an opportunity for you to tell them yours, *unless they ask* . . .

It may be appropriate to share that you, too, have lost a husband, a wife, a parent, a brother or sister, or a child. You can tell them just enough to establish your credentials as someone who is willing to listen and who may have experienced something similar. But beyond that, it is not the time to give them the details of your life . . . *unless they ask.*

And don't tell them, "I know just what you are going through." You don't.

Although you may have experienced something very similar, each individual's experience of grief is unique. Part of their sense of isolation is the feeling that no one else has ever experienced the same thing.

There is a way in which that is true. One of the first things I learned from Elisabeth Kubler-Ross was that each and every individual has a right to experience their grief and/or their death in a unique and personal way. We have no right to take away their denial, their sadness, or their pain. We have no right to expect them to do it the way we would, or the way we feel is most healthy.

Our job is to help them find their own way through.

C. CULTIVATE "SACRED SILENCE"

*Things that are Real
are given and received in Silence.*
MEHER BABA

One of the most useful tools in working with people who are ill or in grief is to learn to be comfortable with another human being in silence, or the cultivation of what Dr. Alan Wolfelt has termed *"sacred silence."*

But one of our culture's most prominent neuroses is a need for continuous stimulation and sensory input.

Just listen to the loud, shrieking, jangled, throbbing beat of the music that accompanies most television commercials, and the theme songs for most television shows—the frantic pace of it all, the driving, relentless intensity. Our school teachers talk about how short our children's' attention spans are. Educators have to become entertainers in order to keep students focused. Attention Deficit Disorder (ADD), a syndrome virtually unheard of twenty-five years ago, has become the new rampant cultural malady.

When I was growing up in the Fifties, we had three television channels. Now there are seventy. And none of them, as a rule, are worth watching.

We make a joke about our obsession with the remote control device. And as a result of some biological quirk, it seems that the human male needs to control access to the remote, as well as what's on the television at any given moment. It has been said that men don't really care *what* is on television. They only care *what else* is on television.

It's easy to see that silence has not been recognized in our culture as an effective tool for social interaction.

But in both spiritual and therapeutic settings, silence is viewed as an extremely important device for establishing inner dialogue and integrating emotional change.

Meher Baba shared an interesting insight about the difference between silence and shouting. He pointed out that two people who are deeply in love usually speak to one another very softly, sometimes in a whisper. But when they are angry, they shout. And the angrier they become, the louder they shout.

The difference, he said, was that when they are feeling deep love, their hearts are "open" . . . it's easy to "hear" each other. And when they are angry, their hearts are "closed" and they feel that they can't "hear" each other.

Cultivating the ability to be in silence with another human being is one of the most useful tools in working with illness, dying, and grief. And it can translate to other aspects of relationship as well.

I originally learned it being with my mother when she was dying. As a result of her brain tumor, she was unable to speak. And I couldn't bring myself to chatter on endlessly about nothing. So we would sit together in silence.

A very precious atmosphere emerged where love and comfort were communicated through our eyes and in our gentle touching and holding of hands. No need for words. No need for newsy chatter or gossip. No need for dishonest reassurances about her condition.

Just pure, unencumbered, heartful, loving silence.

D. LOOKING INTO EACH OTHER'S EYES

We've heard it said that "the eyes are the windows of the soul." Is it possible that, if we look clearly enough, we might actually get a glimpse of someone else's soul or perhaps, in the process, even our own? Seems pretty far out.

But if we learn how to look deeply into another person's eyes without judgment, desire, or expectation, the visions that begin to emerge can be quite remarkable. And the connections we begin to feel can be astounding.

We can see that people's eyes are extremely different. And it's easy to see, within their eyes, the differences in how they relate to others.

Some people's eyes have an opaque quality, a guarded, barrier-like aspect. It's clear they don't want to let you in. They feel constricted, fearful, and isolated.

Others' eyes are wide open. You look in their eyes and it's like looking into an ocean. There is a welcoming, receptive, open quality. They feel vast and huge.

Some are filled with light, a brilliant radiance deep within.

Some are rather dark and muddied.

Some people are trying to overwhelm, control, and manipulate you with their eyes.

Others are just fascinated to see you, to look deeply into you, and to receive you.

AUNT EDITH

Most of us have at least one "scary" intimidating relative.

In my case, it was Aunt Edith.

As my mother's older sister and the eldest of three daughters, Edith took on the role of conservative standard bearer in the family.

Actually, the term "scary" is a bit strong. Edith was very, very sweet and kind. But there was something about her that always made me nervous.

She was religious, steadfast, reliable, and moralistic. She was stern, though her sternness was usually couched in a smile. But her smile, intended to convey warmth, lightness and sincerity, was sometimes a little too taut for my tastes.

I always felt deep love for her. She was my godmother as well as my aunt. But she still made me nervous.

That nervousness only increased as I moved into my rebellious, depressed, surly adolescence. I became everything that I assumed Edith disapproved of.

I dreaded holidays, because I came to expect that each family gathering would involve some degree of moralistic preaching, judgment, and criticism of my lifestyle, musical tastes, wardrobe, and haircut.

*It probably wasn't as bad as I remember it. I was just . . . well . . . **very sensitive.***

For several years after my mother died, I saw little of Aunt Edith.

*But as I moved into my mid-twenties, we began to establish a new relationship. Now **I** was becoming more conservative and was much more receptive to "religious" thought, having done both my undergraduate and graduate degrees in Comparative Religion. Edith thought I had become a "decent" guy. I found her much "sweeter" than I had at an earlier age. We became good friends, and I treasured our friendship.*

When I was in my mid-thirties, Edith suffered a stroke. It turned out to be fairly mild and left her changed in only two ways: She developed a slight slur in her speech pattern and . . . she smiled all the time.

Now Edith used to smile, but, it was often a taut, stern smile.

But her post-stroke smile was beautiful, warm, and radiant. It beamed with child-like wonder, merriment, and delight. Her eyes would get squinty and she would shrug up her shoulders every time something delighted her. And she was frequently delighted.

She became such a pleasure to be around. I never heard her say anything critical or "preachy." She was just a lot of fun.

She seemed to have developed a propensity toward strokes, and continued to have them. Eventually, she and my Uncle Joe had to move into a nursing home together.

With each stroke, Edith lost a little more of her ability to speak.

But with each stroke, she seemed to gain a deeper, clearer connection with her inner beauty.

Her smile was nearly a permanent fixture on her face.

And her eyes, the same crystal blue eyes my mother had, were absolutely radiant. They shone with a penetrating crystalline sparkle unlike anything I had ever seen.

The light coming out of Edith's eyes was nearly blinding in its luminescence.

We say, of course, that the eyes are the windows of the soul. And I've met a number of very "saintly" beings, people whose lives have been centered solely on the development of their connection to God. I've seen some really amazing eyes.

But I've never seen eyes like Aunt Edith's.

In her final two years, her frequent strokes had completely taken away her ability to speak. She could only make sounds like "Ooooooooooooohhhhhhhhhh" or "Aaaaaaaaaahhhhh." And most of her facial muscles were gone. So her mouth hung open and she could no longer smile.

Yet, whenever I came to visit her, I would walk into the room, she would recognize me, and her eyes would brighten. She would "smile" with her eyes. And she couldn't really hug, but she would "hug" me with her eyes.

She was confined to a wheelchair, couldn't speak a word, and could barely move her arms. But I have never received a warmer welcome from anyone than the welcomes I received from Aunt Edith in her final days on earth.

We would sit and hold hands for hours. She would grip my hand with a warmth and sincerity I have rarely experienced. I felt little need to chatter about the events of my life. They seemed pretty meaningless in the face of Edith's predicament. She really couldn't "do" anything anymore. She could only "be." And in her "being" she was incredibly radiant.

So there was little for me to do but just "be" in her presence. We held hands and floated in bliss together. And every time I looked into her eyes, the light was nearly blinding. I knew that through Edith, I was once again getting a little glimpse of God.

The sadly ironic thing is that nursing homes are filled with amazing beings who are often left completely alone. Many people find it difficult to be in someone's presence when they are no longer in full possession of their faculties. I'm sure there were people who avoided visiting my aunt. To them, she was no longer "Edith."

And here she was, a beacon of divinity and holiness, with whom I felt incredibly blessed just to sit in silence.

No, she wasn't the "Edith" we all knew anymore. She couldn't cook, she couldn't talk, she couldn't even smile. She sometimes drooled because she couldn't keep her mouth closed.

But her years of devotion to her spiritual practice had clearly paid off because Aunt Edith, in the years leading up to her departure from her body, was plugged into something unmistakably Divine.

It's interesting. In India there are thousands of beings known as "masts." They may appear, outwardly, to be insane or mentally challenged. They can't care for themselves. They need to be fed, bathed, and taken care of.

Many of them have peculiar habits, small essentially harmless eccentricities that would get them locked up in a mental institution here in America.

But in India they are revered as "saints." It is understood that, for whatever reason, they have established an inner connection with the Divine that has so overwhelmed their everyday consciousness they can no longer function normally. It is considered an honor and a spiritual privilege to take care of such a being.

But in our culture, there is no room for such a concept. We have not made it a practice to connect with the Divine in ourselves and so we have no way of recognizing the Divine in others.

And by "Divine" I simply mean that in each of us which transcends birth, change, and death. That in each of us which is constant, unbreakable, eternal. If you haven't recognized such a place inside yourself, you would do well to make the rest of your life a quest to find it.

Because without it so many precious opportunities are missed, so many amazing and wise beings are ignored because they are in bodies that can no longer function "normally."

We know that many extraordinary souls have transcended the limitations of brain, nerve, and spinal cord damage. There are thousands and thousands of beings like Stephen Hawking, Christopher Reeve, Franklin D. Roosevelt, Helen Keller, Roy Campanella, Stevie Wonder, and Ray Charles who have gone deep inside themselves to unearth awareness, strength, intelligence, and creativity that isn't dependent on their body's ability to function in what our society would perceive as a "normal" way.

We can't help but recognize their greatness.

And there is a similar "greatness" within and around all of us.

But many of us still avoid spending time with someone we love who has gone through such a change, be it the result of an accident, illness, or aging. It's just too uncomfortable. It's too frightening. They aren't the person we "knew" anymore.

Maybe the person we thought we "knew" wasn't them at all.

Maybe the person we thought we "knew" was just the outer shell.

And maybe the person we should get to "know" is the inner pearl . . . the jewel within. The gleaming, glowing, impenetrable inner core that forever remains undamaged and untouched by whatever may happen to the outer shell.

If we learn to touch that in ourselves, we can touch it in others.

Many of us feel imprisoned by our relationships. Many of us suffer because we sense that our loved ones don't really "know" us.

And it's true. Most of the people in our lives project an identity on us that may or may not have anything to do with who we really are. That lack of connection, that lack of feeling truly received and understood, is the source of much grief, resentment, and disappointment in all our relationships.

There is another way in which injured, sick, and aging people make us uncomfortable. They remind us of our own vulnerability. They remind us that we are in bodies that can be damaged, that can and will die.

So our aging and sick loved ones are often left alone, in hospitals and nursing homes, because they aren't who they used to be.

My Aunt Edith wasn't who she used to be. She was happy. She glowed. But she couldn't feed herself. It's an interesting paradox.

Of course, I don't mean to make light of all of this. There is much suffering in sickness, aging, and death. But much of that suffering comes because we have been focused on the "shell" rather than the "pearl."

If we can allow for both the inevitable and the unexpected changes in life, we can be much more capable of loving fully and "knowing" another human being intimately.

Sometimes people avoid visiting loved ones who, like Aunt Edith, are in nursing homes. They avoid it because those loved ones "aren't who they used to be."

And some very precious opportunities are missed . . .

E. EXERCISE

With a close relative, friend, or lover, try the following:

Sit facing each other either in straight-backed chairs or on the floor in the lotus position, with only a few inches separating your knees.

Keep your head, neck, and back in as straight a line as possible without experiencing undue tension.

Take a few deep breaths and breathe out anxiety and tightness.

Focus your eyes on the bridge of your partner's nose, the spot between the eyes. You'll notice that by focusing there you can see both eyes.

Then just relax and gaze into each other's eyes. Don't exert any effort; just look passively, but deeply.

Just keep looking deeper, and deeper, and deeper.

Very shortly you'll begin to see their face changing into a wide variety of personas. You may see angels, animals, and demons. You may see them as old and withered. You may see them as an infant, a child.

Is it your mind projecting on them? Or are you perceiving different levels of their beings in the same way Kirlian photography can perceive the energy fields surrounding human beings?

Who knows?

Just keep looking.

In the center of it all, you'll begin to sense a deepening connection to the core of their being.

It's a fascinating practice.

And for lovers, it can be a blissful, intimate connection unlike any they've previously known.

A recent book about establishing greater intimacy in marriage suggested that lovers try looking into each other's eyes during love-making.

If you can feel comfortable in silence and comfortable gazing for long periods of time into someone else's eyes, you will have two powerful tools for working with dying and grief.

F. Create a Safe Space of Acceptance

I have counseled dying patients and people in grief for twenty-five years. And every now and then, I have worked with someone whose grief was absolutely overwhelming, but whose resolve to find their way through it was inspirational and unforgettable.

In those moments, the only thing we can do for another human being is to create an environment in which they feel safe working through their fears, their hopes, their anger, their pain. We can offer them the reassurance that no matter how difficult what they are experiencing becomes, we will stay with them, if not in body then in spirit. We can let them know that no matter what they say or feel, no matter how confusing or painful it may be for us to witness, we will not judge them and we will not abandon them. This, again, is what Stephen Levine refers to as *"keeping your heart open in hell."*

This level of support often requires that we override what may be habitual patterns of thought or behavior. We are faced with the recognition that our interaction with this being may be their last contact with another human being. We may be the last mirror they look in to get a glimpse of who they are and what their life has been about.

It is a tremendous responsibility that we must bear lightly, but conscientiously. It is up to us whether or not we reflect back to that being divinity or judgment—a spacious awareness into which their spirit can flow and disperse "like ink into water" or a frozen prison cell of our judgments about their life and their resultant sense of diminishment and failure.

CARLOS

I remember one Saturday night back in 1984 getting a call from a fellow named Carlos. A friend of his had given him my phone number. He said, "I wonder if you can help me." He told me he was thinking of committing suicide.

I asked him, "What's happening in your life that makes you feel you want to end it?"

He told me he was gay. All his life he had been ashamed of that. The love of his life had died of AIDS just two months earlier. They had been totally devoted to each other and had lived a quiet, solitary, monogamous life on Staten Island. They had a beautiful townhouse overlooking the water. They had few friends because they were totally fulfilled in each other's company and were completely disinterested in the rampant promiscuity of "the gay scene."

His partner's death was awful to behold, filled with pain, suffering, and despair.

Carlos said that two weeks after his partner died, he discovered that he, too, was HIV positive. His family lived in South America. When he told them he had HIV, they shunned him. It was the first inkling they had about his sexuality and they were a rigidly moralistic Catholic family.

And when his employer found out he had HIV, he suddenly, mysteriously, lost his job.

So he was looking forward to a difficult period of illness followed by a dreary, painful death. And it appeared that he would be forced to do it alone, with no family, no friends, and no money. His heart was shattered. He didn't think he could go on.

He sobbed as he told me his story. Then he gathered his emotions together and asked, "Is there any reason you can think of that I shouldn't commit suicide?"

I was a little stunned. In the past, when I had dealt with people who were suicidal, there was always a much different tone in their voices. Their intent to kill themselves usually felt pathological, sometimes an outgrowth of chronic depression and despair, at other times a panicked reaction to some recent traumatic event.

But Carlos' sobbing felt quite healthy and normal. And when he spoke of suicide, he did so from a very rational, clear, and pragmatic place.

As he spoke, I became overwhelmed by the extraordinary love he expressed for his partner. I, too, was moved to tears. But my tears weren't for Carlos' grief. They were for the rest of the human race, most of whom have never experienced such a pure, all-encompassing connection with another human being.

There are moments in this work when I know that if I am going to be useful to someone, I have to speak to them from my heart. The answers to problems like these don't come from the rational mind.

At those moments, I just close my eyes, quiet my mind, and listen deeply to hear the words that flow from the deepest place I can find in myself.

I began to speak to Carlos about his rare and beautiful capacity to love. I told him how deeply it had moved me. I told him I thought it ironic that he felt shame about his sexuality because I had rarely ever seen heterosexuals who had experienced such profound love and devotion. I told him that he had experienced a precious gift—that in their few years together, he and his loved one had touched a place of pure, unconditional love which few of us touch in an entire lifetime.

I told him that feeling the depth, purity, and profundity of his love over the telephone made me want to meet him in person. If I felt that about him, I knew other people would as well. I told him I couldn't imagine that he would remain alone. His love would be a beacon that would draw others irresistibly into his presence. I told him that the love he felt was what most of us spend our lifetimes reaching for.

I reminded him that although his beloved was physically gone, their love was still very much alive in his heart. And the memories of his loved one were enough to allow him to experience that love. When he experienced that love purely, others around him had the opportunity to experience it too.

Clearly, Carlos' heart was shattered by the physical death of his partner, but at the very same time, his heart was wide open. No container can hold such unbounded love.

I suggested to Carlos that he allow for the possibility of new opportunities. I told him that I felt he would make new friends and find new fulfillment in his life. I invited him to one of our workshops in New York City and we made a plan to meet for dinner a few days later. I suggested that he try giving life a chance. And I promised him that if he failed to find new avenues to happiness and fulfillment within a few months, he would always have the opportunity to end his life.

The next day, during the workshop, we told the 250 participants Carlos' story. Then we told them that he had come that day in order to decide if he should kill himself or not. Without introducing him, we asked what the other people in attendance would like to say to such a being.

There was a stunned, but heartful silence as each participant searched their hearts for words to express their feelings and compassion.

Finally one person got up to speak, then another, then another, until there was a long line waiting for a moment at the microphone so that each could express their love and caring for this stranger in their midst whose identity was a secret, and who had been completely unknown to them just moments before. It was very moving.

Finally, Carlos began to weep. And he wept louder and louder, until he began to wail. We took that to be Carlos' signal that he was willing to reveal his identity to the group.

As soon as the group knew who he was, he was surrounded by love and caring. He made many, many new friends that day and, in fact, embarked on an entirely new life.

We developed a support network for him that helped him to find financial resources, healing resources, and opportunities to deepen his already profound spiritual awareness.

We scheduled meditation groups at his apartment. And as I had suspected, there was never any shortage of people who were anxious to spend time with him. He was a beacon of love, light, and courage, and that love, light, and courage had been awakened through his grief.

If we can allow it to, grief may lead, at times, to an even deeper love and relationship with someone who has died. It's almost uncanny. And that was the case with Carlos. We didn't encourage him to "try to forget" his loved one, but rather to remember more deeply.

After a couple of fascinating years, Carlos gradually developed symptoms and needed more and more frequent hospitalizations. But his new friends all hung in with him and helped him through it.

Finally, about three and a half years after I met him, I got a call from my friend Ganga Stone saying that Carlos was in what was expected to be his "last stay" in the hospital and that I should try to see him.

The next day I walked into his room in the intensive care wing at Sloan-Kettering. An oxygen tank hissed in the corner. Carlos was lying in bed unconsciously tugging at the green transparent mask that covered his nose and mouth, trying to remove it as if it was annoying him. His eyes rotated from side to side. He seemed to be searching over his head for something he couldn't quite see. He was incredibly frail and jaundiced. His skeletal, gaunt face and withered arms shone with a sick, waxy layer of fever and death. He seemed only slightly aware of his surroundings.

I moved first to the foot and then to the side of his bed. I kept looking into his eyes but I wasn't sure he recognized me or was aware I was there.

I moved closer to his side and took his hand in mine. That seemed to capture his attention and he finally focused his eyes on mine.

Then a subtle smile slowly spread across his face and a conscious recognition emerged. He weakly raised his other hand to his mouth and moved his oxygen mask away so he could speak.

It was an effort for him, but for a brief moment he seemed incredibly lucid and clear. "Thank you for everything," he said softly, his Spanish accent as sweet as ever.

I squeezed his hand. He smiled.

We were quiet for a moment and just looked in each other's eyes, searching for the part of us that transcends all the differences and the impending death.

After a few minutes, he again reached up and pulled his mask to one side. "Do you know why I never committed suicide?" he asked.

I said, "No. Why?"

Carlos said, "Because you helped me to see that there was another choice."

I pondered that for a moment.

"Are you glad you didn't?"

Slowly, in halting speech that was clearly an effort, he said, "Yes . . .

very glad. I'm not happy . . . to be so . . . sick. But . . . the . . . last three . . . years have been . . . good."

I thanked him for staying around so all of us could get to know him.

A few more quiet moments passed. Then he said, "But . . . now . . . I . . . want . . . to . . . get . . . out . . . of . . . this . . . body!"

I said, "Carlos, it looks like that's going to happen very soon."

He said, "Good . . ."

Then he seemed to start drifting away again, so I seized a precious opportunity. "By the way," I said, "I love you."

He smiled. "I love you, too."

He died a couple of hours later.

I will never forget Carlos. His love was awesome, his heart so pure . . . like those of a great saint.

I think it was his openness, his honesty, and his willingness to be vulnerable that gave him the ability to transcend his broken heart and learn to love life again.

Too many of us feel we need to numb ourselves emotionally. And too many of us feel that our sadness would be an imposition on others, so we hide it.

But Carlos was willing to experience it fully and to share it. He was an extraordinary blend of mind and heart He danced clearly and courageously on the edge that separates chaos from cosmos . . . heartbreak from wisdom.

As Thomas Merton said, *"True prayer and love are learned when prayer has become impossible and the heart has turned to stone."*

There is no doubt in my mind that Carlos knew in the depths of his soul what true prayer and love are. He was an inspiration to all of us.

The only thing I ever did for him was encourage him to recognize his own awesome capacity for love.

The only thing I ever gave him was the opportunity to experience and to trust in what he already knew, and who he already was.

G. TUNING TO YOUR INTUITION

It is difficult to talk about intuition. Our culture has seldom understood or discussed it. And there have been few, if any, methods given to us for learning how to connect with it.

To me, intuition is our pipeline to the Divine; it's the voice of God. It's the channel through which we hear the highest wisdom we can hear.

When I am speaking from "intuition," I often have the sense that the words are not coming from my mind but from something much higher, much deeper.

The "purest" intuition has nothing to do with me or my thinking, rational mind. And the "best" things I have ever said felt like they came "through" me rather than "from" me.

At an earlier time in our history, intuition was perceived, somewhat disparagingly, as a feminine quality. The only time we would hear the term was when we heard about "women's intuition." It was as if the real method of perception, done by men, was *thinking*.

Fortunately, those rigid gender-based notions have begun to fade away. And our "irrational" worship of the rational mind has begun to loosen its grip somewhat.

After all, no less a thinker than Albert Einstein told us that he did not come to his understanding of the fundamental laws of the Universe through his rational mind. He "just had a feeling."

If one of the greatest minds of the twentieth century found another way of "knowing," perhaps the rest of us might benefit from a similar awareness.

And most of us have, from time to time, felt that we "just have a feeling" about something. My father used to call it "a hunch." And great, powerful, tough businessman though he was, he always maintained that his biggest accomplishments and successes in business came when he listened to his "hunches."

The *Star Wars* movie series portrayed many scenes in which the great "Jedi" warrior, Obi-wan Kenobi, seeks to teach his student, Luke Skywalker, the principles of becoming a successful Jedi warrior. "Feel the Force, Luke . . ." he would say, "Go with the force."

The "Force" is an invisible, ever-present, subtly perceptible field of energy which would always direct the Jedi warrior to success in battle and to accomplishment of the ultimate good.

Likewise, our intuition is always available to us. We merely need to spend some time cultivating our awareness of it.

And I know of nothing that is of greater use in working with people who are grieving than intuition.

In order to most effectively "hear" our intuition, we need a quiet mind. The meditation practices we spoke of in Chapters Twelve and Seventeen are an invaluable resource in helping us achieve that "quietness."

When the mind becomes quiet, intuitive thoughts can rise to the surface. It's almost like those old black fortune-telling balls they used to sell in joke and novelty shops, the ones with a small window on the bottom. When you turn them upside down, a short phrase or "fortune" rises to the surface and becomes visible in the window.

Likewise, a word, phrase, idea, or feeling rises up when we are quiet and open to our intuition. We can say it . . . or not. We can act on it . . . or not. But there it is.

Sometimes I find that intuition gives rise to some pretty radical or "far-out" thoughts. And often, in the context of working with grief and/or dying, if I have spoken the thoughts as they came into my mind, they have broken through an otherwise "frozen" or stifled atmosphere. They have opened a doorway to a new, deeper communication. They have brought laughter or a perceptible lightness to an otherwise oppressive situation.

When those intuitive thoughts are *really* good, they have opened the door to an enlightened perception which had previously been ignored, or had seemed inaccessible.

Each time I go to visit with someone who is dying or in grief and every time I give a lecture or workshop, I try to sit quietly for at least ten minutes prior to getting out of my car or entering the lecture hall or hospital room. I just find a quiet place, sit down alone, quiet my mind, and open, so that there is, hopefully, a greater possibility of something really healing and really useful coming through me.

Not ideas, but love and wisdom.

DIANA

Despite the many years I have been doing this work and the months of preparation leading up to Diana's death, I still felt a wave of shock run through me when the hearse drove up to the church.

I had arrived early and was sitting in my car using the cell phone to catch up on calls.

Suddenly, there was that long black car, and I gasped.

"Here she comes," I said to my colleague on the other end of the phone. "I have to go."

It was a brand new hearse, shining in the bright sun of early autumn. The setting was peaceful . . . pastoral. The church was surrounded by farms and rolling hills. The trees, mostly verdant summer greens, also displayed subtle glimpses of yellow, red, and orange . . . the first hints of fall.

The chill in the air was a strange contrast to the warmth of the sun.

And the heavy, leaden, inanimate box the pallbearers rolled out the back door of the hearse was a strange contrast to Diana's lightness, her radiant love, and brilliant awareness which felt so alive in my heart.

Her parents and brother were following the hearse in her mother's Lincoln. They were solemn, as one would expect . . . but not overcome.

Her mother had left a message on my answering machine thirty-six hours earlier: "Diana died this morning. We're doing fine. We'll be going out to dinner and then to bed early. You can call tomorrow."

Her death was not a surprise. For months Diana had kept an answering machine of her own next to her bed so that even when she didn't feel well enough to talk, those of us who kept in touch could leave a message.

But, for ten days prior to her mother's call, there was nothing . . . no tape of Diana's sweet voice saying, "I'm not able to answer the phone now. But I'd love to know you called. Please leave a message and I'll call you back as soon as I can."

Nothing . . .

Just endless, unanswered ringing.

And I, the experienced companion to folks leaving their bodies, nevertheless felt empty, apprehensive, and even slightly desperate.

In just a few months I had become very attached to this radiant beacon of devotion and love.

I finally surmised that her condition must have worsened dramatically, and her parents had removed the phone and the answering machine from her room.

Her mother and father were extremely private people and in all my months of visiting had never given me their own unlisted number.

They lived a great distance out in the country, on a large, wooded estate. The long, winding, private road that weaves its way through the woods to their beautiful, impeccably maintained home is wonderfully picturesque, often surrounded by herds of deer, flocks of geese, and wild turkeys.

But there were some creatures Diana's mother didn't want around. She had recently seen a bear on the property. It wasn't welcome.

And I don't think I would have been if I had dropped by uninvited.

So I stayed away, the only option for communication being inner dialogue with Diana during my meditations.

She had originally been referred to me by Stephen and Ondrea Levine. Ondrea had called one day about six months earlier. She described Diana as "a real sweetheart" and suggested that since she was in New Jersey, perhaps I could visit her.

"She's very sick," Ondrea said. "She's forty-four years old and has fifth stage breast cancer. She probably won't live more than a few more months. She's a Kripalu yoga teacher from Massachusetts. She's gone home to her parents' house in New Jersey. But she's feeling lonely and isolated because most of her friends are in Massachusetts."

So I called Diana and made an appointment to visit her a few days later.

It's interesting how different people bring out different sides of our personalities. With Diana, from our very first phone conversation, I always felt drawn to my deepest, most intuitive, spiritual awareness.

I have never been with anyone who so clearly witnessed her own life and death as "passing show."

What I mean is, she wasn't all that attached to it as something real. She felt the feelings. She experienced the emotions. She felt the pain. She cried and periodically fell into depressions. But ultimately she would laugh, a deep, playful, giggling laugh that expressed all of the extraordinary spiritual awareness she had cultivated over the past twenty-five years. Diana, perhaps more than anyone I have ever worked with, knew that she wasn't her body.

But as we worked together, there were a few things which came up where clearly she was caught.

She was frustrated that, although she had been deeply committed to her yoga practice and taking care of her health for years, her physical condition now made it impossible for her to do the postures. Since much of her practice of tuning to God was done through her yoga postures (asanas), she felt a little adrift spiritually.

Also, she had been divorced a few years earlier from a man she deeply loved who, according to Diana, had suddenly left her one day for a younger, more beautiful woman. Diana's cancer was discovered about six months later.

And despite Diana's protests, he refused to come back when she became sick and refused to postpone the divorce proceedings although she had to appear in court during the worst days of her chemotherapy treatments.

She said, "I will never understand how he could leave and how he could treat me so coldly when I was so sick. We had a perfectly wonderful relationship. And although he knows I am dying, I haven't heard from him since we were divorced."

On my fifth or sixth visit, she asked me if I'd like to see her tumor. She had shown me a photograph of it on my second visit, but now, in a gesture of self-revelation and intimacy, she was moved to unveil "the real thing."

It was startling. What I had thus far seen as a large protrusion on her upper chest under a puffy blanket of sterile surgical dressings was, in actuality, an enormous growth of sinister, deranged, hyperactive cells.

It was huge, black like charcoal, implanted in her chest like a large football, a black, lumpy football jutting at an angle up out of her chest just beneath the collarbone, above where the right breast used to be. It was dry-looking, with crusty, craggy canyons and valleys punctuated by small pools of yellowish-green oozing pus.

As I quieted my turbulent mind, I watched many, many layers of horror appear and then disappear. In twenty-two years of doing this work, no one had ever shown me anything even remotely close to the level of diseased disfigurement this beautiful woman had revealed.

I have often seen photographs of cancerous lungs in anti-smoking literature. And I have been with many people who had been in horrible accidents, had been burned, had wasted away from the ravages of cancer and AIDS. But I had never seen anything like this.

*I said, "Boy, Diana, when you grow a tumor, you **really** grow a tumor!"*

And the foul, fetid stench of the massive necrotic tissue was overwhelming.

One day we were reflecting on attachment and irony. Diana said, "Isn't it amazing that I have spent my entire life loving good smells. I love flowers and perfumes and incense. I love fresh air and the smell of the ocean. I was even a practicing aromatherapist . . .

"And now I get to spend my final days with this horrible stench pouring out of my own body from a huge lump that sits just under my nose."

I took all that in.

"I wonder what it means?" she puzzled.

I closed my eyes and quieted down, listening as deeply as I could to hear some inner wisdom

I remembered a story about the great Indian spiritual teacher, Meher Baba. A little girl had once approached Baba and asked, "If God is all beautiful and all-loving and all-powerful, why is there evil and suffering in the world?"

And Baba answered, "Well, you, my dear, are a very, very beautiful girl. And you are a very good girl. But when you sit on the toilet each day, you bring forth that which is foul and stinking. In the same way, God who is all-beautiful also brings forth that which is not beautiful. It is just a law of Nature, when spirit comes into form."

I told this story to Diana.

And then I said, "Diana, dear, I'm sorry to have to report that my beautiful body is also filled with horrible smells. Just spend an evening with me after Indian food or onion soup. You wouldn't believe it!"

We both laughed.

And she said apologetically, "But I'm sorry you have to experience mine."

I said, "Just be thankful you haven't had to experience mine!"

And again we laughed with delight.

At a later date, she let it slip in conversation that her ex-husband had a tendency to be selfish, self-centered, and emotionally unavailable. And Diana admitted that she was often "difficult" in the relationship.

"So it wasn't really perfect," I said.

"Well, no, I guess not," said Diana.

I listened, for a moment, to the inner quiet.

Finally, I said, "You know, Diana, I think in the next few weeks you might do some work on forgiving your ex-husband. Because I think, as a result of the chronology, that there is a subtle way in which you are blaming him for your illness. And, I think, that you and I both know that is off the mark.

"You would be doing yourself a great service to forgive him, and realize that he is just another confused human being with his own inner problems to contend with. He really had nothing to do with your cancer . . .

"I don't know why you have cancer, and you don't know why, but I suspect that intuitively you will find some profound teaching that all of this is leading to. And I suspect that, whatever that teaching is, it will include the awareness that God is not just to be found in a beautiful relationship or in a strong yoga practice or in beautiful fragrances and a healthy body, but God is everywhere, even in your smelly old tumor, right under your nose."

We both sat quietly with all that for some time.

The next time I visited her, she told me she had decided I was right. She had worked for several weeks to clear out whatever resentment remained. Finally, when she felt she had really reached clarity, she called her ex-husband and left a message on his answering machine telling him that she forgave him and that she wished him a happy life.

The next day he called back and he and Diana had a wonderful, healing conversation.

That's what we refer to as "finishing business."

She also had a crisis of faith. Her parents were both devout Catholics, but Diana had opted to find her way spiritually through yoga, meditation, and a variety of Eastern spiritual teachers.

Now she was unable to do yoga and because of the pain medications she was taking had little ability to meditate. She also felt that her spiritual teacher had abandoned her in her darkest hour.

Finally, Diana called me one day in tears. As most of the trappings of her spiritual life had fallen away, she had one last tool she clung to: A favorite Sanskrit mantra, "Om, namo bhagavate vasu devaya," which loosely translated means, "May I surrender to the will of the Lord."

Diana was beginning to drift in and out of consciousness for longer periods each day and at one point, in an effort to maintain some sense of continuity in her spiritual practice, she asked her mother if she would be willing to repeat the mantra in Diana's presence for a few minutes each day.

But her mother was unwilling. Diana was crushed. Her mother is a Roman Catholic. She was uncomfortable reciting a Hindu phrase.

*In her final days, Diana was still clinging to a subtle hope that her parents would know, appreciate, approve of, and embrace her spiritual path. And although her father had several times taken her to visit her Indian spiritual teacher, Diana felt he didn't **really** understand what it was all about. She longed, as many of us do, to feel fully "accepted" and "understood" by her parents.*

But our parents live in different worlds. They come from different generations. Their life experiences are vastly different than ours.

I tried to think of something that would convey to Diana the perfection in her mother's response.

So I quieted for a moment. Suddenly, I remembered another great story. I related it to Diana.

The story dealt with a Buddhist teacher who was challenged by a student for not scrupulously following his own teachings. Ultimately, the master said to the student, "You should be grateful for the shortcomings in your teachers. They remind you that the Buddha is nowhere to be found but within your Self."

I said to Diana, "There is still a subtle way in which you are looking for approval from your parents. It's like looking for God in external people, or actions, or things. Obviously, God is everywhere, in everything and in everyone. God is in your mom, and your dad, and your brother. And if God is perfect, their actions are perfect.

"But it seems that all of this is a fierce teaching in finding that God is within your own Self; that it has nothing to do with whether or not you can do yoga, or meditate, or repeat your mantra. It has nothing to do with what your mother or your father or anyone else says or feels. It doesn't look like you're being allowed the leeway to feel safe in anything less than the deepest Truth you know . . ."

The last time I saw Diana, there was little left to talk about. She had worked through a lot of her issues with her ex-husband, her family, and her spirituality. She was relatively weak, in a lot of pain, and pretty zonked-out from the morphine.

But she smiled so peacefully . . .

Finally, I asked if I could rub her feet.

She said, "That would be lovely. But don't you want to wash them first?"

"My hands?" I asked with a quirky, puzzled giggle.

"No, silly, my feet!" she giggled back.

"Why?" I asked, "Are they unusually dirty?"

She said, "No, I don't think so. I'm just so used to feeling diseased and contaminated."

"Well, unless you've been frolicking in fields of cow dung, I think I can risk it."

At moments like these I always try to remember Mahatma Gandhi's phi-

losophy. When he worked with lepers and people with smallpox, others would warn Gandhi that he was exposing himself to the diseases. Gandhi would simply say, "If God wants me to get leprosy or smallpox, then I will get leprosy or smallpox. But if he wants me to do this work, then he will protect me."

As I began to rub her feet, we drifted off into a beautifully intimate, silent space that was punctuated by some very playful banter.

She said, "My mind keeps getting confused."

I said, "That's because you're all hopped up on drugs. Or maybe you're just going crazy. Which do you think it is?" I laughed.

"The drugs," she said.

"Oh sure," I shot back, "You drug fiends always want to blame it on the drugs. You'll never admit that you're really insane!"

She said, "I'm sure that this foot rub is wonderful, but I'm not sure I'm really feeling it."

"It's those damn drugs you're taking! What do you expect?"

She laughed. The irony was, she was so committed to good health she would never have taken recreational drugs. And it was fun to play a little bit with the absurdity of her predicament.

Finally, I said, "Whatever we do, let's try to have it bring us both closer to God."

And Diana said, "I always feel closer to God when we're together."

It was one of the nicest things anyone had ever said to me.

Finally, when it was time for me to go, I hugged her and said, "Well, my love, vaya con Dios."

Diana smiled. She said, "You go with God, too"

About two weeks later, she died.

And on the day of her funeral, I felt her presence so strongly . . .

And I felt her smiling, knowing that it no longer felt necessary to her that her parents embrace, understand, or accept her spiritual beliefs. Eventually, she was happy just to know that they would be comforted by what was familiar to them.

The Roman Catholic funeral Diana's parents held was the perfect way for them to honor her, to remember her, and to begin the process of healing their own sadness.

But Diana was a much bigger being than any religion could ever hold. She had, as had Thomas Merton, Mother Teresa, Father Bede Griffiths, and others, transcended the boundaries of Roman Catholicism and the boundaries of Hinduism. Her life and her death had continuously pushed her to know the Universal God, beyond all definition.

I was quite convinced that Diana had many times tasted Heaven while she was on earth. I even felt that I had tasted a bit whenever I was with her.

She was a great blessing and a great inspiration to me and to all who knew her. Her faith, dignity, and humor, and her willingness to experience her humanity fully are unforgettable.

She has become a part of the fabric of my being.

Chapter Twenty

THE "I" OF THE STORM

> *Healing is not forcing the sun to shine, but letting*
> *go of that which blocks the light.*
> STEPHEN AND ONDREA LEVINE

So THOSE WE LOVE BECOME A PART OF US. AND EACH RELATIONSHIP, each encounter, each interaction, and every love become important threads woven into the quilt of our beings.

On and on it goes. At times, it's difficult to feel the connections we so long for. At other times, we wish we didn't feel them.

Over the course of our lives, each of us has a set of experiences that can open us to deeper and deeper levels of love and awareness . . . if we allow them to.

Ironically, *every loss gives us the opportunity to experience ourselves, and our lives more deeply, and more fully.*

We *fear* loss because of what it takes away.

But we *honor* loss when we recognize its ability to peel away the layers of who we *think* we are.

Then we can experience who we *really* are.

We *think* we are our bodies, our minds, our personalities, our thoughts, our possessions, our accomplishments.

We *really* are spiritual beings . . . glorious, radiant fullness . . . unbounded love . . . insightful awareness . . . intuitive peace . . . profound compassion.

It's astonishing.

We are created in the image of our Creator.

And throughout our lives, we've gotten a little glimpse here, a little scent there, a moment of insight, a moment of familiarity, a subtle recognition, each in its own way showing us the magnificence of who we really are.

And then, most of us forget about it, because we don't have much support for that kind of awakening in this culture.

The losses in our lives offer us amazing opportunities:

We can fall victim to despair and resentment.

Or we can transform the despair and resentment into fuel for our inner journey . . .

Most of us know the power of despair and resentment. They can consume us like a raging inferno.

But, like that inferno, they can also propel us outward and inward, as rocket fuel propels spacecrafts toward heaven.

Each relationship, no matter how beautiful or how difficult, is a gift.

The beauty in the relationship helps us touch our *inner beauty.*

The difficulty in the relationship lets us confront that which keeps us separate from our *inner beauty.*

And what keeps us separate from our inner beauty is all within ourselves . . . It's the dark corners of our minds that tell us we are not enough, that delude us into thinking we need external people and situations to be a certain way in order to feel safe, fulfilled, and complete.

There is no one in our life who will always behave the way we want them to.

And there is no one in our life who will always be there when we want them to be.

And there is no one in our life who is protected from the inherent dangers and changes of form.

There is no money which cannot be lost.

There is no possession which cannot be broken, or moth-eaten, or rusted, or faded, or stolen.

And there is no safety other than that which we hold in our own hearts . . . in our own souls.

Our safety is there . . . within us . . . ever-present, throughout our lives . . . patiently waiting to be recognized and set free.

THE EYE OF THE STORM

As a child, I spent two summers on the beach just south of Atlantic City.

One evening at the end of the summer of 1960, we found out that Hurricane Donna, which had been swirling around in the Caribbean and Florida, was suddenly roaring up the Eastern Seaboard. She was predicted to hit our area around dawn.

It was too late for us to leave so my mother, my sister, and I resolved to try to "ride it out."

And it was one of the most awesome and fearsome experiences I have ever had.

The wind howled like a giant crazed dragon. It blew with a strength and ferocity I had never seen before. It became dense, no longer airy, with a solidity like rock. We couldn't push our door open.

And the force pushing against the door didn't feel like wind. It felt like a huge boulder blocking the door. It wouldn't budge. Not an inch. We were trapped inside our apartment for several hours during the height of the storm.

The ocean rose high and mighty, roaring and pounding relentlessly. It swallowed nearly 100 yards of sandy beach for miles to the north of us and miles to the south of us. Huge, monstrous waves were breaking over the boardwalk. Each time they receded they tore away large sections of the boardwalk like a lion tearing flesh from a carcass.

Great frothing sheets of white foam formed on top of the waves. The monster wind ripped them away, blowing them free to spray forth in showery torrents of painful pelting droplets.

The sky was ominously dark and dreadful. The street in front of our apartment, normally 125 yards away from the surf, became flooded with ocean water.

I sat for hours, watching through the window in awe as the sweet summer environment I had known for years now sustained an onslaught of unimaginable proportions. Windows cracked. Great jagged sheets of glass sailed across the sky, shattering against the street, the walls, the trees. Roofs of houses were torn away. Window shutters careened through the air like deranged, apoplectic birds. All sorts of indistinguishable debris hurtled madly, erratically through the darkened, chaotic sky, crashing against anything in its path, and smashing to smithereens.

The wind roared, the rain poured, the ocean became an awesome, monstrous force of incomprehensible fury.

And I sat fascinated . . . perhaps even a little bemused. I could never have imagined the immeasurable power I was witnessing—the raging fury of Nature in a frenzy of thoughtless destruction.

I was awed by its beauty . . . and unrestrained raw power.

*And I was awed that it didn't frighten me. Because I couldn't perceive any ill will or evil intent. The storm just was, as winter, spring, summer, and fall **are**. I had no sense of Divine rage, wrath, or punishment raining down from the heavens.*

It was just one of Nature's cycles.

It didn't set out to damage things, to kill people, to displace them from their homes.

It was just what it was.

A great, big, powerful storm.

Doing what great big, powerful storms do.

It had no intent.

It meant no harm.

And I felt strangely safe . . . protected because I sought not to challenge it or judge it.

I felt honor, appreciation, awe, and respect.

After several hours of mind-boggling chaos, the wind and rain slowly began to diminish. The sea became calmer. The insatiable waves began to recede.

Finally we could open our door.

And finally, it was safe to go outside.

What amazed me more than anything else was the blue sky and sunlight that suddenly appeared, and the peaceful, quiet calm that emerged in the wake of the danger and destruction.

I had nearly forgotten that there was still blue sky and sunshine behind all the darkness, chaos, and danger.

And then, after an hour or so, again the storm returned. And there was more fury and devastation.

And then, again, it receded . . .

Hurricanes, the most dangerous and destructive forces in Nature, have at their core a circle, perhaps twenty to thirty miles in diameter, of calm, sunlight, and serenity. This circle is known as the "eye" of the storm, a vast, tranquil, open space around which the cyclonic storm swirls.

In the "eye" there is no wind. No rain. No clouds. No destruction. The sun shines.

There is peace.

It's a fascinating phenomenon.

In the center of the most violent, raging, destructive force in Nature, there is quiet . . . calmness . . . serenity.

In the months and years following a loss, we feel as though we're caught in an emotional storm. We are consumed with a sense of swirling, unpredictable danger . . . a profoundly unbalanced agitation . . . an unrelenting anxiety.

But we have forgotten that we also have a calm center. In this case, the "I" of the storm.

We have forgotten that at the core of our beings is a detached, dispassionate awareness that watches it all with equanimity.

It is the part of us that never changes.

It is the part of us that transcends death.

It is the part of us we call our "soul."

But, like many other things our modern, technological society has ignored, our spirits . . . our souls . . . have been neglected for centuries.

We hardly even know we have them.

We read about them in holy books, but, we don't really know them. Our popular religious traditions have left us with few methods for consciously recognizing their presence within us.

But there are little glimmers throughout our lives.

In Chapter Seventeen, we made reference to those moments in the middle of a terrible argument with a loved one when we hear a little voice inside saying, "Isn't this ridiculous?!"

At those times we sometimes fight against our inclination to dissolve into laughter . . . we may be suddenly impelled to hug, kiss, and forgive the offender.

There's a part of us watching it all from another vantage point.

At times of extreme danger, we may notice that there is a dispassionate awareness watching our fear . . . watching our minds freak-out . . . giggling with a recognition that our terror is almost laughable.

Virtually everyone I've ever spoken to who has experienced a sudden, unforeseen "accident" or frightening turn of events has reported that they noticed a calm awareness from which they were watching it all without fear.

It's as if at moments of sudden shock or great stress our minds burn out momentarily and allow our consciousness to dissolve, however briefly, into the pure, undifferentiated, peaceful awareness of our souls.

It's somewhat akin to the reports of people who have had "near death" experiences, who sometimes talk about witnessing their consciousness rising up out of their bodies and hovering overhead as they watch and listen to events unfolding in the room below—the doctors and nurses scurrying to resuscitate them, the panic, the hopelessness, the resignation, sometimes even jokes that are told in the room.

And then they return and report, to the doctors' and nurses' astonishment, that they were aware of everything that was said, and everything that happened while they were "dead."

As these events unfold, we notice that if fear does arise, it often arises after the fact.

At the height of danger, our consciousness stays clear and calm.

We *calmly* watch our car spinning out of control on ice. Only after it *stops* do we dissolve into terror as our minds "replay" the danger we just avoided.

At a moment of danger, we may see our entire life flash before our eyes in a millisecond.

But as it happens our minds are calm.

We touch this state of serenity during moments of profound joy or at moments of unaccustomed tranquillity, like the moments we spoke about in Chapter Twelve when we are sitting by a river, or the ocean, or on a mountaintop . . .

One friend feels it when he is trout fishing, standing waist-deep in the center of the stream . . . aware only of the water moving against his legs, the breeze, the gentle swaying of the leaves in the trees, the singing of the birds.

Another feels it in his boat, out at sea, with no land in sight, no other boats in sight, just the swelling of the waves and the interplay of wind and sail.

Another feels it when she is scuba diving . . . entering another world . . . a world of vast silence . . . and radiant, pulsating, shimmering beauty.

Throughout our lives, that inner place has been there, but it's been ignored.

When we touch it, it comes as a surprise.

We don't recognize it.

We think of it as an aberration.

That state of calm, dispassionate awareness is always available to us. And, with a little practice, at any moment, it is possible for us to tune to that inner place . . . to recognize it . . . to hear its wisdom.

It is the place meditation can take us.
It is the place contemplative prayer aligns us with.
It is the place tai chi attunes us to.

Each of these methods and many others seek to familiarize us with that which lies at the core of our beings, that which is eternal, unchanging, ever-present, that which, in the end, is the only thing that can truly satisfy us, sustain us, nurture us, and fulfill us.

*It is the place we are **really** seeking when we "fall in love."*

And it is the place we need to connect with to integrate all of life's inevitable losses into our beings.

Our society, in its zeal to "protect" us from suffering, has actually created a kind of emotional and spiritual paralysis. And that paralysis has inhibited our ability to see and perceive things *as they are.*

Because, things *as they are* have seemed too frightening.

*The way things **are** is only frightening when we have no awareness of a "higher" power.* It is only frightening when we have no awareness of a transcendent reality that is timeless and cannot die, and no awareness of our connection to it.

Once we begin to gain that awareness, we can look directly at our lives without fear. We can look at the reality that everything in form is impermanent. Everything changes. Everything decays and dies.

The curse of being human is that our rational minds always seek to "understand," to make rational sense of something that is, by its nature, completely beyond the mind's ability to grasp.

But we keep trying. We keep attempting to understand how God or the Universe can, at times, seem so cold, so heartless, so cruel . . . how life in form can seem so chaotic.

The *blessing of loss* is that it offers us situations in which the pain is so devastating, the sequence of events so confusing, we are "thrown" out of our minds.

The *hope* is that we will come to understand that our minds cannot "think" us back to peace and contentment.

We *can* begin to "feel" our way through, to instinctively sense the other levels of awareness and existence within ourselves. *And in that instinctive feeling, we can find the part of us which transcends death.*

And when we find it, we recognize its Oneness with the part of our loved ones that transcends death.

It's the same thing.

What is found in our loved ones is found in ourselves.
It's our connection to our heart.
It's our connection to each other.
It's our connection to our Creator.

Like the "eye" of the hurricane, the "I" within each of us, within the often chaotic storm of human life, sits quietly and serenely at our core.

A sailor unexpectedly caught in a hurricane knows his only hope is to find the eye, sail to it, and remain inside it, moving within the storm, at its center, until it subsides. It may take days—even weeks—of vigilant effort. But, within the "eye," while the raging storm swirls all around him, both he and his craft will be safe.

And, confronted with the terrible devastation of loss, what choice have we but to sail into our "I?" To find our own souls. To connect with the highest and deepest spiritual awareness we possess.

We need only find ways to approach our "I," to recognize it, and to learn how to connect with it.

To "reside" in it at will . . .

It is the transition from thinking to intuition.

It is the journey from the mind to the heart.

It is the unveiling of our soul.

It is the rebirth that death and loss offer us.

May we all recognize the silver lining
In each dark cloud . . .
The "I" of the storm.

OTHER BOOKS TO READ

Tuesdays with Morrie by Mitch Albom (Doubleday)

The Essential Rumi by Coleman Barks with John Moyne (Castle Books/Harper, San Francisco)

How to Survive the Loss of a Love by Melba Colgrove, Harold H. Bloomfield, and Peter McWilliams (Prelude Press)

Journey to Ixtlan by Carlos Casteneda (Pocket Books)

Prayer is Good Medicine by Larry Dossey, M.D. (Harper/Collins)

Your Erroneous Zones by Dr. Wayne W. Dyer (Harper)

Your Sacred Self by Dr. Wayne W. Dyer (Harper)

Sometimes My Heart Goes Numb by Charles Garfield (Jossey-Bass)

The Experience of Insight by Joseph Goldstein (Shambala)

Living When a Loved One Has Died by Earl A. Grollman (Beacon Press)

Connect by Edward M. Hallowell, M.D. (Pantheon)

The Courage to Laugh by Allen Klein (Tarcher)

The Healing Power of Humor by Allen Klein (Tarcher)

Freedom From the Known by J. Krishnamurti (Harper)

On Death and Dying by Elisabeth Kubler-Ross (Macmillan)

The Wheel of Life by Elisabeth Kubler-Ross (Scribner)

The New American Spirituality by Elizabeth Lesser (Random House)

A Gradual Awakening by Stephen Levine (Doubleday)

A Year to Live by Stephen Levine (Bell Tower)

Embracing the Beloved by Stephen & Ondrea Levine (Doubleday)

Guided Meditations, Explorations, and Healings by Stephen Levine (Doubleday)

Healing Into Life and Death by Stephen Levine (Doubleday)

Meetings at the Edge by Stephen Levine (Doubleday)

Who Dies? by Stephen Levine (Doubleday)

Everyday Enlightenment by Dan Millman (Warner)

How Can I Help? by Ram Dass and Paul Gorman (Knopf)

Journey of Awakening by Ram Dass (Bantam)

How To Go On Living When Someone You Love Dies by Therese A. Rando (Bantam)

The Tibetan Book of Living and Dying by Sogyal Rimpoche (Rupa)

Start the Conversation by Ganga Stone (Warner)

Zen Mind, Beginner's Mind by Shunryu Suzuki (Weatherhill)

The Journey Through Grief by Alan D. Wolfelt (Companion Press)

Understanding Grief by Alan D. Wolfelt (Accelerated Development)

INDEX

ABOUT THE AUTHOR

JOHN E. WELSHONS IS THE FOUNDER AND PRESIDENT OF OPEN HEART SEMINARS, an organization born in 1981 and dedicated to enhancing spiritual education and awareness in our society.

Since the early 1970's, John has spent much time working with his friends Ram Dass, Stephen Levine, Pat Rodegast, Judith Stanton, Dale Borglum, and others setting up lectures, workshops, and retreats, many of which have been focused on people who were terminally ill and people in grief. He says his life was "dramatically changed" by his first meeting with Dr. Elisabeth Kubler-Ross in 1976.

He is a frequent lecturer to businesses, churches, synagogues, hospitals, colleges and universities throughout the United States, and has done extensive counseling with dying patients and people in grief. He is working on a number of writing projects and has a series of cassette tapes and booklets on grief which are available to the general public. Some of John's tapes have been developed in conjunction with his good friend, Mark Victor Hansen, co-author of the best-selling *Chicken Soup For The Soul* book series.

John holds a B.A. in Religious Studies from the University of South Florida and an M.A. in History of Religions from Florida State University where he taught "Death and Dying." He has also taught at Ramapo College in New Jersey.

From 1983 to 1996 he served as president of a mid-size corporation in New Jersey. He has twice traveled to India to study the rich religious and cultural traditions there, and has traveled extensively in England, France, Italy, and the former Soviet Union.

He is available for lectures, workshops, and seminars, and can be reached by contacting:

OPEN HEART SEMINARS
P.O. Box 110
Little Falls, New Jersey 07424
Phone: (800) 555-0844 toll-free
Fax: (973) 256-4260
www.openheartseminars.com

OTHER OFFERINGS FROM OPEN HEART PUBLICATIONS

HEALING THE GRIEF (...of the loss of a loved one)
by
Mark Victor Hansen & John E. Welshons
....$18.95
(Two 90-minute audio cassettes)

TAPE ONE *of this extraordinary set contains a conversation between best-selling author MARK VICTOR HANSEN (Chicken Soup for the Soul, The Aladdin Factor, Dare to Win, Out of the Blue, etc.) and noted grief counselor, JOHN E. WELSHONS, President of Open Heart Seminars. Mark and John offer the listener a variety of techniques for working through the sadness, despair, confusion, and numbness that usually follow a significant loss in our lives. Many people have found, after a couple of listenings, that they begin to move into a new perspective on the experience. They begin to see the possibility of healing and growing once again into wholeness.*

TAPE TWO *contains further explorations into how to move through loss into wholeness and fullness. It contains a series of step-by-step recommendations for working with the experience of grief and also offers two guided meditations for reconnecting, through the heart, with loved ones who have died. It gives guidance on healing hurts and bitterness through the magic of forgiveness.*

BEGINNING MEDITATION
(Calming Your Inner Self)
by John E. Welshons
....$10.00
(One 60-minute audio cassette)

Most of us would like greater peace, greater clarity, greater aliveness, and greater love in our lives, yet we know little about how to calm our minds, especially when our lives are difficult and painful. With extraordinary clarity, this tape offers a simple and effective introduction to MINDFULNESS MEDITATION, a practice that can be done daily to bring wisdom, fullness, and gentleness back into our lives.

QUICK ORDER FORM

Fax Orders: (973) 256-4260 Send this form.

Telephone Orders: Call Open Heart Publications toll free at
                           (800) 555-0844. Have your credit card ready.

On Line Orders: www.openheartseminars.com

Postal Orders: Open Heart Publications
                           P.O. Box 110
                           Little Falls, New Jersey 07424 USA
                           Telephone: (973) 256-5015

Please send the following books and / or tapes:

Quantity	Item		Total
_____	Awakening from Grief (book)	@ $14.95 each =	_____
_____	Healing the Grief (tapes)	@ $18.95 each =	_____
_____	Beginning Meditation (tape)	@ $10.00 each =	_____

Sales Tax:
New Jersey residents please add 6% sales tax for product shipped
to New Jersey addresses.

Shipping in U.S.:
$4.00 for the first book or tape and $1.00 for each additional book
or tape.

Please send more FREE information on:
❑ Other Books & Tapes   ❑ Speaking / Seminars
❑ Mailing List   ❑ Consulting

Name: _____

Address: _____

City: _____ **State:** _____ **Zip:** _____

Telephone: _____

e-mail address: _____

Payment: ❑ Cheque   ❑ Credit Card:
❑ VISA   ❑ Master Card   ❑ AMEX   ❑ Optima
Card Number: _____

Name on Card: _____Exp. Date: _____

Signature: _____

QUICK ORDER FORM

Fax Orders: (973) 256-4260 Send this form.

Telephone Orders: Call Open Heart Publications toll free at (800) 555-0844. Have your credit card ready.

On Line Orders: www.openheartseminars.com

Postal Orders: Open Heart Publications
P.O. Box 110
Little Falls, New Jersey 07424 USA
Telephone: (973) 256-5015

Please send the following books and/or tapes:

Quantity	Item	Total
_____	Awakening from Grief (book) @ $14.95 each =	_____
_____	Healing the Grief (tapes) @ $18.95 each =	_____
_____	Beginning Meditation (tape) @ $10.00 each =	_____

Sales Tax:
New Jersey residents please add 6% sales tax for product shipped to New Jersey addresses.

Shipping in U.S.:
$4.00 for the first book or tape and $1.00 for each additional book or tape.

Please send more FREE information on:
❏ Other Books & Tapes   ❏ Speaking/Seminars
❏ Mailing List   ❏ Consulting

Name: _____

Address: _____

City: _____ **State:** _____ **Zip:** _____

Telephone: _____

e-mail address: _____

Payment: ❏ Cheque ❏ Credit Card:
❏ VISA   ❏ Master Card   ❏ AMEX   ❏ Optima
Card Number: _____

Name on Card: _____Exp. Date: _____

Signature: _____

Quick Order Form

Fax Orders: (973) 256-4260 Send this form.

Telephone Orders: Call Open Heart Publications toll free at (800) 555-0844. Have your credit card ready.

On Line Orders: www.openheartseminars.com

Postal Orders: Open Heart Publications
P.O. Box 110
Little Falls, New Jersey 07424 USA
Telephone: (973) 256-5015

Please send the following books and/or tapes:

Quantity	Item		Total
_____	Awakening from Grief (book)	@ $14.95 each =	_____
_____	Healing the Grief (tapes)	@ $18.95 each =	_____
_____	Beginning Meditation (tape)	@ $10.00 each =	_____

Sales Tax:
New Jersey residents please add 6% sales tax for product shipped to New Jersey addresses.

Shipping in U.S.:
$4.00 for the first book or tape and $1.00 for each additional book or tape.

Please send more FREE information on:
- ❑ Other Books & Tapes
- ❑ Mailing List
- ❑ Speaking/Seminars
- ❑ Consulting

Name: _____

Address: _____

City: _____ **State:** _____ **Zip:** _____

Telephone: _____

e-mail address: _____

Payment: ❑ Cheque ❑ Credit Card:
❑ VISA   ❑ Master Card   ❑ AMEX   ❑ Optima
Card Number: _____

Name on Card: _____Exp. Date: _____

Signature: _____